Y0-BCL-024

Marrying
in the
Church

Marrying in the Church

A Pastoral Guide

to Canon XXI of the General Synod
of the Anglican Church of Canada,
issued under the authority of the
Sub-Committee on Marriage and
Related Matters.

Graham Cotter
editor

Anglican Book Centre
Toronto, Ontario Canada

1983
Anglican Book Centre
600 Jarvis Street
Toronto, Ontario
Canada M4Y 2J6

Printed in Canada

Canadian Cataloguing in Publication Data

Marrying in the church

ISBN 0-919891-06-3

1. Marriage counseling.   2. Marriage - Religious
aspects - Anglican Church of Canada.   3. Marriage
(Canon Law).   I. Cotter, Graham

BX5149.M2M37   1983   248.4'837104   C83-098813-0

Contents

Foreword

I am grateful for the opportunity to write a letter of commendation for this pastoral guide to Canon XXI "On Marriage in the Church" for two reasons in particular:

First, because this Canon was developed with great care and much prayer over a number of years, to help our church move from what was felt by many to be primarily a legislative approach to persons and marriage to a pastoral approach — one that required knowledge and understanding on the part of all. This change has not always been understood in our church.

Second, because, as I set forth in a brief presentation at the 1978 Lambeth Conference, I am convinced that today we are called upon both "to uphold basic Christian values and at the same time to minister with love and concern to those who fail to live up to these standards, and to do so in a way that does not create a sense of condemnation or rejection."

One essential step in doing this, in the realm of marriage and the family, is to help people come to an understanding of what are some of the basic Christian values relating to marriage. Canon XXI and this guide are important resources to help clergy and laity together to achieve deeper understanding and insight in this area.

I commend the pastoral guide and trust it will be carefully studied and wisely used.

Edward W. Scott,
Primate,
The Anglican Church of Canada

Questions for the user of the guide

Revision of the Canon is under consideration, and improvements to this pastoral guide are always welcome: to assist in this process, would you please answer these questions and return your answers to

> The Reverend Tom Kingston,
> Church House, 600 Jarvis Street,
> Toronto, Ontario
> M4Y 2J6

The above is also the person to whom other questions and comments on the Handbook are to be addressed.

1 After using this Handbook, have you found it helped in guiding you through the Canon? If so, in what ways?

2 Please comment on the pastoral emphasis in the introductory chapter.

3 Does the Canon itself work well for you? Are there parts of the Canon you particularly agree with, or parts that you would like the General Synod to change? Please specify.

4 The questions and answers in chapter 3 arose from the use of the Canon. Are there other questions whose substance is not covered here that you would like to have answered? If so, what are they?

Introduction

The Sub-Committee on Marriage and Related Matters originally asked the Reverend Dr Charles Feilding, former dean of divinity and professor of Pastoral Theology at Trinity College, Toronto, to prepare this guide. Dr Feilding began the task, but illness and death intervened in 1978, and it fell to me to follow the instructions of the sub-committee.

In doing this, I was able to draw on the existing writings of Charles Feilding and of Stuart Ryan, professor of Law at Queen's University and chancellor of the Diocese of Ontario. In particular, I used their joint publications, *Marriage in Church and State* (Toronto: Anglican Book Centre, 1965) and the previous commentary on the first version of the revised Canon (*On Marriage in the Church*, Toronto: Anglican Church of Canada, Department of Christian Social Service, 1965).

In addition, I had at my disposal questions and answers already published by the sub-committee and its predecessor, the Commission on Marriage and Related Matters, dated 22 October, 1975; in response to questions from the Diocese of Niagara, "Some Fundamental Principles of Canon 21", 17 January 1977; in response to the Diocese of New Westminster, 11 March 1977; and another 17 March 1977.

The sub-committee has been a very creative context in which to work over the past five years, and the tone of intelligent concern for the care of marriage and the family has been set, above all, by Charles Feilding and Stuart Ryan, who have been, more than the rest of us, the authors of the Canon and the commentary here presented.

The guide is intended to be used by clergy and others who are preparing couples for marriage or counselling on marital concerns. It is designed to help the incumbent see the value of the time he spends responding to pastoral needs relating to marriage, to explicate the text of the Canon, and to list questions which have arisen about the Canon.

At the time of printing, the sub-committee is preparing to offer workshops in the ecclesiastical provinces and dioceses of Canada, where these are requested, on the meaning and use of Canon XXI. The guide is a prime requisite for the conduct and the success of these workshops. The editor and the sub-committee hope that the people who are most concerned about marriage in the church will use the guide, the workshops, and whatever means of communication they wish, to allow the sub-committee to be most useful in service to the church.

Graham Cotter

Who Officiates?

This guide is designed to assist those who are involved in preparation for marriage, the solemnization of marriage, the planning of weddings, and the pastoral care of those who are married, including those whose marriages have broken down.

The Sub-Committee on Marriage and Related Matters believes that the good news of Jesus Christ is good news for marriage, and that the church's ministry of Holy Matrimony is a vital celebration of that good news in the relations between men and women. Those who prepare others for Christian marriage and plan and solemnize weddings are, ultimately, the Christian community, whose affection, guidance, and support are needed by married couples. But specifically the tasks fall on the ordained ministry, those referred to in our marriage Canon as "incumbents." The word *incumbent* in its origin means "leaning on," and a fair modern interpretation in this context is that the parish ministers should expect to be "leaned on" by those who come for pastoral care. It is incumbent upon the incumbents to respond to the needs of the people.

Who Is the Incumbent of a Parish?

An incumbent is one who has been called and sent to become a pastor in a place where he or she has been duly instituted by authority of the bishop of the diocese. He or she is authorized to exercise pastoral functions in a *parish* which is normally a more or less defined district within a more clearly defined area called a *diocese*. Diocese and parish are both terms of geographical reference. Following this usage, a *parishioner* is one who lives in a parish, whether or not he or she is a member of an Anglican congregation in that parish, or even a Christian. Strictly speaking, people are not members of a parish but residents in a parish. However, in common usage the two expressions *parishioner* and *member of a congregation* have become confused. In the same way, the words *incumbent* and *pastor* tend to become confused and sometimes identified in popular usage.

For many Anglicans, the incumbent of the parish where they live is the same person as their pastor; but this is not necessarily so. Not everyone has an accessible pastor or even a pastor at all. Everyone, however, resides inevitably in a diocese and must therefore reside in some area where the bishop is himself the incumbent or has designated an incumbent. And it is to this incumbent that an application under the Canon must be made: an "applicant" must apply "to the incumbent of the parish or mission where it is desired that the intended marriage be celebrated" (*Canon XXI*, Part IV, 1(B), cf. also Part III, 3(C)2).

The place where it is planned or hoped that the marriage may take place, be it noted, is *not* defined as where an applicant has worshipped or will worship. In many cases persons immediately go to live far from the place where they were married. In other cases in our mobile society, people are often married far from the original home of either of them, the place of the wedding being chosen for reasons of present employment, the avoidance of excessive travel costs, etc. An application is directly related to a geographical factor, rather than to an existing personal or pastoral relationship.

The principle to be upheld is the divine calling of the church to minister to all manner of people and not merely to practising Anglicans.

(To extend this principle, where there is no incumbent and no parish, the canon makes special provision for members of the armed services for whom otherwise the rules might be impossible to follow. Also, among Anglicans generally, it is now customary to treat all members of a congregation as *canonically resident* within its parish boundaries.)

12

In view of all this, the applicant does not have so much to know a pastor as to approach the appropriate incumbent. In these circumstances, applicant and incumbent may never have met before. In our highly mobile society, this becomes more and more likely, and the church is fortunate in having kept alive a system of parishes and incumbents to whom all residents of an area can expect to have access, even when there is no one whom they think of as their pastor. The call of the incumbent is to become the pastor of such people even if only for a short time at a critical moment in their lives.

An incumbent's duties are potentially to all who live in the parish. These duties he or she shares with the bishop who assigned them at induction: "Accept this charge which is mine and thine." The bishop's duties are likewise toward all who live in his diocese. This general principle is made abundantly clear at the "Consecration of Bishops" (Canadian *Book of Common Prayer*, pages 663f) where "all . . . within his Diocese," including not only the "poor and needy . . . and . . . all strangers destitute of help" but even "gainsayers" and the "criminous" are designated as objects of his concern. It is this ministry which every incumbent is called to share in his or her particular area of the diocese. Therefore, the fact that applicant and an incumbent may not hitherto have known each other is not unexpected and is certainly no bar to application. The incumbent, as we have said, by this firmly grounded canonical tradition, is here given the opportunity of becoming the pastor he or she was called or sent to be.

An incumbent therefore stands in the great tradition of the gospel and of the mission of God to all humankind. Not merely the employed minister of a sect or religious society paid to serve its members, the pastor is designated as one whose potential mission is to all who live within the assignment. An incumbent working under this lofty charter can ill afford to turn away any resident or potential resident

13

who asks for help, unless it is to introduce a caller to another and more appropriate incumbent or other helper.

Clearly, in this tradition, an applicant cannot be turned away merely because he or she is unknown to the incumbent or congregation. Nothing in the Canon could justify such a procedure, besides which it would be contrary to the gospel. Of course, it will not always be possible to satisfy all the desires of every particular applicant for marriage, or to make a favourable report upon every application. The incumbent is also under obligation to deal with the application in accordance with the Canon and with the usual principles of pastoral practice and, in the case of application for remarriage after divorce, to forward any completed application to the ecclesiastical matrimonial commission together with a report upon it.

The Initial Encounter with Applicants for Marriage

While it is widely held that stability of residence by families in a community is generally desirable, this is no longer possible for an increasing number of people. It used to be said that a long pastoral ministry in one place helped a pastor to become familiar with families' problems over much of a lifetime, allowing for more help in times of crisis. The likelihood of such an experience is now becoming rare. This situation is particularly relevant to a pastor's sudden and unexpected encounters with applicants for marriage previously unknown. How many pastors have been tempted to dismiss such applicants without further ado, as unwarranted intruders upon their pastoral work with "their own people"?

How might these initial encounters be turned into creative pastoral relationships? What are the motives and resources in the Christian tradition available to the pastor for this work? These are large and important questions. Here we deal briefly with only two elements of a possible answer: particular aspects of the gospel as a source of

14

motivation; and canon law as a guide in the education of conscience, rather than as a compendium of rules to be blindly obeyed.

Subsequent or Future Meetings with the Couple

We have already drawn attention to the incumbent's call to become a pastor. Our aim is to encourage further reflection on certain aspects of the gospel, as a source of motivation for pastoral counsel with applicants for marriage in the context of the present-day parish and incumbency.

In every human encounter, even with a total stranger, there is available to the mind of the believer the good news that God himself is present in the encounter: "I was a stranger and you welcomed me."

It is an attitude illustrated by images that ground it in the structure of the universe, in the reality of the divine life itself: "You will be sons of the Most High; for He is kind to the ungrateful and the selfish." Sun and rain are images of the God whose fatherly love extends to all. This love, described in this way, is active and present. It is, as it were, the atmosphere we are given to breathe or in which, failing to breathe, we shall wither. It is an atmosphere in which either we find life, or become exposed as empty.

It is this insight about the nature of God, this *revelation*, which lies at the heart of the Christian ethic. The Christian ethic is good news before it is good advice. No Canon law, no bishop, no congregation can abrogate the duties which flow from acceptance to the revelation of the gospel, and which include duties to serve the unlovely, the ungrateful, and the stranger.

The love of strangers as a particular virtue was greatly honoured in the creative community of the first Christians. Its meaning has been partly obscured for readers of the English Bible where the Greek word for it has usually been rendered as hospitality. This is a virtue or moral capacity which is obviously required in a community that proposed to grow by uniting to itself those who are strangers to its faith. The duty which its gift entails is prior to the Canon; the canon rests upon its exercise and, incidentally, prepares a welcome for some who are strangers to the Christian faith (Part II, 3) and for others who are strangers to the Anglican Church.

We now draw attention to a classic passage in the New Testament: "If you love those who love you, what credit is that to you? For even sinners love those who love them" (Luke 6:32-38). A form of care planned for our own people and at the expense of strangers, as familiar saying has it, must fall under this judgment whether engaged in by congregations or by their leaders.

To take the position we have just outlined is not to assume that every request for marriage in the church should be granted; but it does assume that every applicant is to be welcomed, and every request treated thoughtfully and with respect. The thoughtful and courteous refusal of a request can be the beginning of a creative pastoral relationship; it can be the friendly direction of an applicant to a more appropriate resource, with care to make the introduction; and finally it can mark a step in the maturing of conscience. It is to this last possibility that we now turn.

The Mysterious "Third Party" Ever Present

A contemporary philosopher-theologian, reflecting on the practice of counselling of all kinds, once observed that in every relationship of this kind, two always meet in the presence of a third. Who or what is this mysterious third? To the Christian believer, the reference may seem to be obvious: it is God, revealed in Christ. But the third here has a wider reference, and is applicable in every counselling encounter regardless of the religious faith of the participants.

Present in every encounter, for example, are assumptions that the participants bring about what each believes to be real, what each believes he must somehow reckon with in the long run. This may, of course, be a world in which forgiveness, growth, and the power of a new life are available. But for others it may be an essentially evil world in which the only obligation is to survive at any cost. Or again, it may be a world in which some familiar expression such as "business is business" conceals a rejection of honesty and justice as viable characteristics of a fully developed human life in accord with reality.

On the other side, the counsellor may harbour, consciously or unconsciously, views of what is attainable, desirable, necessary, ideal, or whatever — something he believes commands attention. For the counsellor this also is some part of the third. Likewise, the applicant may bring an image of something or someone who he too sees as commanding attention. An applicant may take it for granted that the counsellor (in this case perhaps the incumbent) shares a view of reality. On the other hand, he or she may assume that the counsellor opposes it. In one instance an inquirer may, as it were, imagine the ten commandments posted on the wall behind the counsellor; more subtly, an applicant may feel commanded by the voice of a mother as heard in childhood having now forgotten its source. Again, it may be the expectations of society, associates, or family which seem to reflect an unalterable account of reality — of whatever is believed at this moment and must ultimately be reckoned with.

What is proposed here at initial interviews is neither a short course of psychotherapy or counselling, nor a life-long education of conscience; it is only the need for a deep awareness on the part of the pastor of the beginning of their journey, *as the couple sees it.* Many couples will "do the right thing for the wrong reason" and a longer time will be needed for reassessment of reasons — perhaps a lifetime. A pastor must accept what is found and begin from there, not from the world of textbooks. Seldom, if ever, are couples versed in the theology of marriage or of its Canon law. More likely the incumbent will meet people concerned about their very identity as human beings (though they will not put it that way) — an important subject to ventilate should they propose to marry. It is by paying close attention to whatever the couple brings to the interview that the pastor, and perhaps they, may discern their opening upon the world of faith. It may be an opening not labelled with theological or even vaguely religious language. They may want a church wedding for a purely secular reason. Should the way be opened for a disclosure of grace? Or should it be barred? How sure are we of the ways of God, one of whose properties has ever been to astonish? Are we also of little faith?

In any initial encounter, even with persons who are known, there must be at least these two elements which are attended to. First, a welcome which springs ultimately from the source of the counsellor's faith — what the pastor believes about the world in which the encounter takes place. Second, a deep determination to understand what is being asked for behind the apparently simple question as to performance of the marriage rites (i.e. a determination to perceive the "third"). Is the proposed marriage an excuse to escape an intolerable situation? Is it a "shotgun" wedding? Is it a temporary madness of romance? Is it for social approval? Is it something long brooded over, openly discussed, and maturely arrived at? At least some preliminary answers to questions such as these (not necessarily answers put into words) will be needed in the incumbent's mind before a decision can be made, whether to offer help and clarification, or to assist the applicant in finding some more appropriate help. The rescue of a harrassed applicant from a marriage he or she does not really want is one of the possible outcomes that might be borne in mind!

These comments have been strictly confined to only two elements that should be present at initial interviews. The marriage education that may be needed later is a subject not undertaken here.

If the incumbent decides in due course to establish a continuing pastoral relationship to arrive at some major decision about a potential marriage, answers to certain questions posed by both the civil and the Canon law will be necessary. The pastor might need to have in mind the application forms associated with Parts III and IV of the Canon. More frequently, obvious questions will emerge in pre-marriage counselling. How old are you? Where were you born? What is the nationality of your parents, or your cultural background? Have you been married before? Are you baptized? How long have you known each other? Do you belong to a church? Does your family approve of your marriage? Have you made a budget? Where are you going to live?

Any such questions, and there may be a hundred more, asked one after the other, machine-gun fashion, in some arbitrary order, would of course ruin any possibility of serious counselling. This is not the way to secure useful and truthful information. It is, instead, an interrogation, a method associated with the sanctions of a police court, a passport office, or a personal loan office. In purposeful pastoral interviewing most of the information needed will emerge in the order in which the applicants offer it and the pastor prepares the ground for it. Forms, when needed at all, are first of all guides to the pastor as to the scope of the interview. When the needed information has emerged and been discussed, in whatever order, and has taken a mutually agreeable form, it will not be difficult to enter it on the forms or in the registers.

Throughout the whole of this process, the pastor and the applicants are together in the presence of another significant third, namely, marriage itself: its human and transcendent character, the civil and canonical requirements for it, the obligations it entails, the joys it offers, and the divine support it is promised. The pastor is not the source of these elements which make up the third but, like the applicants, must recognize them, assess a relationship to them, and be subject to them. Counsellor and applicant

19

are, as it were, side by side contemplating the third together.

The true counsellor (the incumbent becoming pastor) is not one who is to say, "I'm telling you"; rather the pastor is one who helps the applicant to look at all the factors which bear on the decision to marry in the church, and to suspend judgment until having done so. These constitute a reality which they must look at together, which binds them both, and which is liable to become obscured if in its place the pastor substitutes personal judgments, however elegantly they may be obscured by so-called discretion.

Notes

1 It should be emphasized that while the incumbent is obliged to receive and listen to those who request to be married, no pastor is required to marry any couple who do not qualify, who are unprepared or, in the pastor's view, uncommitted.

2 There are parts of Canada where the idea of parish "territory" will hardly be applicable; in such cases, as in others where applicants for marriage do not live within the known territorial parish of the incumbent, the pastor acts under the authority of the diocesan bishop. The emphasis on territorial incumbency in this chapter is intended to stress, first, that all of Canada is within the area of the church's responsibility (all dioceses *are* territorial, even if some parishes may not be); second, that all Canadians have some right to expect pastoral care from a church with this universal presence.

What are the Rules?
Canon XXI
with Commentary

What is the Canon?

A canon, as passed by the General Synod of the Anglican Church of Canada, sets out the standards by which the corporate church life is to be ordered. The word canon is primarily associated with the ordering of a Christian community as a fellowship of the Spirit.

Canon in Greek means a stick or rule, as in the English *yardstick*. Its one significant New Testament use for our purpose is in Galatians 6, 15:

> For neither circumcision nor uncircumcision matters; what matters is a new creation; and for those who run their lives by this canon, peace be upon them and mercy, and upon the Israel of God.

Here canon means "according to this plan" or "on this model": the model is Christ's human life which ended on the cross; it is also the work of the life-creating Spirit which reproduces that life in the believer; that life is the new creation.

Canon in this passage is not an ordinance or a law, but a model, a life to be imitated, and a response to the life-giving Spirit who makes the imitation possible; this is a model not only for the individual, but also for the community, and the true community can be identified by the quality of its life and faith which in turn depend on faithfulness to the model.

The model or plan itself is dependent on the standard embodied in the person of Jesus Christ. The calling of the individual Christian and of the Christian community is to make life an imitation of him.

To accomplish this, the Christian uses those means by which the likeness of Christ can be found for living out his or her life: prayer and communion with God, the reading of the Bible and other holy writings, and the example and counsel of fellow Christians, both as individuals and as the corporate church.

To find the likeness of Christ through Holy Matrimony, the church offers its canon on *Marriage in the Church*, to guide the behaviour of its members in marriage and related matters as it affects their life in Christ. This canon is the public rule of the church which sets out how marriage can be entered into, maintained and restored, within the life of the church and as a means for the imitation of Christ.

The Requirements of the Canon for Christian Marriage and Related Matters

1 The Canon defines the marriages to which its rules pertain. This definition is found in the preface, paragraphs 1–5.

2 The Canon states the duties of Christian people, pastors and others, respecting the welfare of those who are married and of those whose marriage is imperilled or broken: in the preface, paragraphs 6, 7, and 8.

3 The Canon defines what is required of those who seek marriage in this church: in text, Part I; "The Prerequisites for Marriage."

4 The Canon prescribes how the contract of marriage in the church is to be made: in Part II, "The Solemnization of Matrimony."

5 The Canon defines the status in the church of any who request the rites and sacraments of the church when there is reason to believe that their marriage or purported marriage to one still living may not be a marriage

as defined in the Canon: Part III, "Determination of Marital Status under this Canon."

6 The Canon defines the status of any who seek remarriage in the church after civil divorce from one still living: in Part IV, "The Remarriage of a Divorced Person whose Former Partner is still living."

7 The Canon defines the status in the church of any who seek admission or readmission to Holy Communion when there is reason to believe that their existing marriage may not be in accordance with canonical discipline: in Part V, "Admission to Communion in Special Cases."

8 The Canon provides for the establishment of a Commission with authority to determine whatever is required under 5 and 6 above: in Part VI, "Ecclesiastical Matrimonial Commission." The Canon further sets forth under Part VII, "Forms" means by which the Ecclesiastical Matrimonial Commission can function in an orderly and standard manner when providing assistance to those mentioned in 5 and 6.

On Marriage in the Church

The Title

The words *On Marriage in the Church* identify the church as the sphere of the Canon's major concern. In relation to marriage the Canon is an instrument of the church's pastoral care of the people of God both in their life together in the church and in their mission to the world.

Preface

1   The Anglican Church of Canada affirms, according to our Lord's teaching as found in Holy Scripture and expressed in the Form or Solemnization of Matrimony in the Book of Common Prayer, that marriage is a lifelong union in faithful love,

for better or for worse, to the exclusion of all others on either side. This union is established by God's grace when two duly qualified persons enter into a contract of marriage in which they declare their intention of fulfilling its purposes and exchange vows to be faithful to one another until they are separated by death. The purposes of marriage are mutual fellowship, support, and comfort, the procreation (if it may be) and nurture of children, and the creation of a relationship in which sexuality may serve personal fulfilment in a community of faithful love. This contract is made in the sight of God and in the presence of witnesses and of an authorized minister.

The four sentences define respectively the *status* of marriage, the *contract* that establishes the status, the divine *purpose* of marriage, and the essential elements at present required in the *ceremonies*.

The status of marriage is seen as good in Holy Scripture and in the Solemnization of Matrimony in the *Book of Common Prayer*. The preface and the definition of marriage in the declaration (see page 00) must be taken in conjunction with the definition of marriage as found in the Prayer Book. Since new rites are permitted from time to time, new definitions in such rites must be compared with the meaning in the 1959 version and in the relevant parts of the Canon.

The *contract* derives from two sources: God's grace, and mutual consent. Mutual consent is the fundamental requirement for human marriage agreed upon by western civil and Canon law. The contract is sometimes referred to as a covenant, a word of good scriptural precedent. For example, the new marriage rite of the Episcopal Church in the U.S.A.: "The bond and covenant of marriage which was established by God in creation."

The essential elements in the ceremonies include the conscientious and open acknowledgement of God's presence, the witnesses, who represent the community of Christians (see clauses 6–8, below) and the authorized minister who, in practice, represents both church and state.

2   The Church affirms in like manner the goodness of the union of man and woman in marriage, this being of God's creation.[1] Marriage also is exalted as a sign[2] of the redeeming purpose of God to unite all things in Christ[3], the purpose made known in the reunion of divided humanity in the Church.[4]

1   Cf. Gen. 1:27–31.
2   Eph. 5:31f.
3   Eph. 1:9f.
4   Eph. 2:11–16

1   Genesis 1:27–31

"So God created man in his own image; in the image of God he created him; male and female he created them. God blessed them and said to them, Be fruitful and increase, fill the earth and subdue it, rule over the fish of the sea, the birds of heaven, and every living thing that moves upon the earth."

(Genesis 1:29–31 continues the theme of God giving man his place in creation, and of this blessing of man. Note that "man" is in twofold form, male and female; Genesis 1 does not subordinate one sex to the other.)

2   Ephesians 5:31f.

"Thus it is that (in words of the Scripture) a man shall leave his father and mother and shall be joined to his wife, and the two shall become one flesh. It is a great truth that is hidden here. Some refer it to Christ and the Church, but it applies also individually."

3   Ephesians 1:9f.

"He had made known to us his hidden purpose — such was his will and pleasure determined beforehand in Christ — to be put into effect when the time was ripe: namely, that the universe, all in heaven and on earth, might be brought into unity in Christ."

(Verses 11–12 point out that the Gentiles were at one time separate from Christ.)

"Your world was a world without hope and without God. But now in union with Christ Jesus you who were once far off have been brought near through the shedding of Christ's blood. For he is our peace. Gentiles and Jews, he has made the two one and in his own body of flesh and blood has broken down the enmity which stood like a dividing wall between them; for he annulled the law with its rules and regulations, so as to create out of the two a single new humanity in himself, thereby making peace. This was his purpose, to reconcile the two in a single body to God through the cross on which he killed the enmity."

The reason for citing these passages is to show that marriage is both an example of the movement in God's creation toward divine union, and is a sign of that greater unity toward which God is bringing all things through the healing and unifying power of the cross.

3.   The Church throughout her history has recognized that not all marriages in human society conform, or are intended to conform to the standard here described. For this reason, in the exercise of pastoral care as evidenced in the earliest documents of the New Testament, the Church has from the beginning made regulations for the support of family life especially among her own members.

Clause 3 is an explicit justification for development in Canon law from New Testament times, and guards against literalism in interpretation. (Cf. Article XX of the XXXIX Articles, of the authority of the church.)

This clause reminds believers that the Canon law does not necessarily coincide at all points with the law of the civil community. The reminder is necessary in a post-Christian society because for a long time, in earlier days, the Canon law alone controlled marriage or was identical with the civil law, so that people came to think of both as one in purpose and origin. Already while the New Testament was being written, the church had begun to differentiate its own marriage discipline from that of the Palestinian and Graeco-Roman communities in which its members lived. In England, on the other hand, especially after the sixteenth century, much common law doctrine entered into Canon law simply by inattention; the present Canon is a step toward clarification.

4. Aspects of the regulation of marriage in the apostolic Church are recorded in the New Testament. A new standard of reciprocal love between husband and wife was introduced leading towards an understanding of their equality.[1] In preparation for marriage Christians were directed to seek partners from among their fellow believers.[2] In Christ's name separated spouses were encouraged to seek reconciliation[3]. In His name also divorce was forbidden though not without exception.[4] In certain circumstances a believer already married to an unbeliever might be declared free from such a marriage bond[5]; in others, and here in the name of Christ, remarriage during the lifetime of a former spouse was described, with one exception, as an adulteorus union[6].

Clause 4 establishes the authority for the church's regulation of marriage among its members by citing virtually all the known details of that regulation in New Testament times. By giving specific references, the legislative authority of the church can be seen at work in the historical context of its beginnings and can be seen, therefore, not to be something arbitrary or whimsical but open to investigation.

1   1 Cor. 6:3f, 11:11f, Eph. 5:21–33, cf Gal. 3:28

The equality of husband and wife.
1 Corinthians 7:3f

"The husband must give the wife what is due to her, and the wife equally must give the husband his due. The wife cannot claim her body as her own; it is her husband's. Equally, the husband cannot claim his body as his own; it is his wife's."

1 Corinthians 11:11f

"And yet, in Christ's fellowship woman is as essential to man as man to woman. If woman was made out of man, it is through woman that man now comes to be; and God is the source of all."

Ephesians 5:21

"Be subject to one another out of reverence for Christ."
    Ephesians 22–30 develops the responsibilities of husband and wife for each other, concluding with the great analogy between marriage on the one hand, and the relation of Christ and the church on the other. See clause 2, note 2 above.

Galatians 3:28

"There is no such thing as Jew and Greek, slave and freeman, male and female; for you are all one person in Christ."

2   1 Cor. 7:39, 2 Cor. 6:14, cf 1 Thess. 4:2–8

Marrying fellow believers
1 Corinthians 7:39

"A wife is bound to her husband as long as he lives. But if the husband dies, she is free to marry whom she will provided the marriage is within the Lord's fellowship."

2 Corinthians 6:14

"Do not unite yourselves with unbelievers; they are not fit mates for you. What has righteousness to do with wickedness? Can light consort with darkness?"

See also Thessalonians 4:2–8, a passage on keeping the body holy.

3   1 Cor. 7:10f.

1 Corinthians 7:10f

"To the married I give this ruling, which is not mine but the Lord's: a wife must not separate herself from her husband; if she does she must either remain unmarried or be reconciled to her husband; and the husband must not divorce his wife."

4   Matt. 5:31f, Mark 10:2–9, cf. Mal 2:13–16.
5   1 Cor. 7:12–16
6   Matt 19.9, Mark 10:11f, Luke 16:18, cf. Ro. 7:3.

For a discussion of these passages see the commentary on Part IV of the Canon.

5.   From these principles and precedents the Church, living in many cultures and in contact with many different systems of law, has sought in her rites and canons to uphold and maintain the Christian standard of marriage in the societies in which believers dwell. This standard and these rites and canons pertain to the selection of marriage partners, preparation for marriage, the formation of a true marriage bond, the solemnization of marriage, the duties of family life, the reconciliation of alienated spouses, and to the dissolution of marriage and its consequences.

Clause 5 makes it clear that the New Testament regulation of marriage was the beginning of a living tradition, not the end of a dead one.

6   All members of this Church, in fulfilling the obligations of the People of God, share according to their circumstances in the obligation to uphold Christian standards of marriage in human society, especially by care for their own families and by neighbourly care for the families of others. Special obligations rest upon certain members of the Church as set forth below.

7   The particular duties of the clergy, described in part elsewhere in this Canon, include the provision of education for marriage and family life, the solemnization of marriage, the pastoral care of families, the encouragement of reconciliation of estranged spouses, and the pastoral care of those whose family ties have been broken or interrupted by death, sickness, poverty, enforced absence, human weakness, or by wilful act.

8   The duties of the laity, according to their several circumstances, are to share with the clergy the responsibility for upholding family life, in particular —

A   By their presence with friends and neighbours at weddings to bear witness to their support of those who marry,

B   To safeguard the legality of marriages by readiness to allege promptly any cause or just impediment which might make a proposed marriage unlawful,

C   To promote and encourage the use of the professional skills that serve family life,

D   As spouses, to be faithful to their own marriage vows,

E   As parents, guardians, god-parents, teachers, or other duly qualified persons, to guide children and young persons in preparation for family life,

F   As neighbours, mutually to promote the welfare of families, and to seek the reconciliation of any whose family life is impaired or broken,

G As communicants, to uphold the Church's discipline, and to seek the restoration to communion of any who have become alienated or are excommunicate,

H As citizens, to work for the maintenance of just laws for the welfare of family life.

Clauses 6, 7 & 8
Obligations of the People of God

It is unfair to place the entire weight of responsibility for maintaining a Christian marriage and home on an isolated couple. The church lays particular stress on the importance of faithfulness in lifelong union "for better for worse, for richer for poorer, in sickness and in health." When therefore families are afflicted by poverty, illness, or "worse," the church has a corresponding duty to stand by them with both material and spiritual aid. This duty must be discharged in many ways and through various agencies, including agencies of the civil society to which church members also belong and in which they share responsibility. Particular duties fall on particular individuals, including both laity and clergy; indeed, even the best pastors can discharge only a small part of this total responsibility, however significant their contribution may be. Besides the help of friends and neighbours, many professionally trained people are normally required to give the necessary assistance when family ties are threatened, or when they have been interrupted or broken by death, sickness, poverty, enforced absence, human weakness, or by willful act. Members of the church are to be found serving in all these capacities both neighbourly and professionally. They include physicians, lawyers, teachers, social workers, and many others. It is quite as proper that their duties as Christians should be referred to with respect in Canon law, as it is that the duties of pastors should be singled out. The duty of pastors to aid in the reconciliation of estranged spouses is frequently referred to in ecclesiastical statements of great moral authority; the duty of pastors in the work of reconciliation generally is specifically referred to in the rubrics printed before the "Order for Holy Communion" in the Prayer Book. Rubrics and Canons should not lend support to grandiose ideas about pastoral work to the exclusion of the duties of doctors, lawyers, and others, which they too may perform as duty bound by their Christian profession, as well as by their respective professional standards.

Part I
Prerequisites for Marriage
1 Notice

It shall be the duty of those who intend to marry to give notice to the minister at least thirty days before the day proposed for the wedding, except that the minister may at his discretion waive this requirement for sufficient cause in which case he shall notify the bishop of the diocese in writing, stating the reason for his decision.

The requirement in clause 1 of due notice is necessary if preparation for marriage is to be undertaken seriously. The Canon proposed in England imposes upon the minister the duty of instruction, but imposes upon the applicants no corresponding duty of giving notice. To avoid difficulty in exceptional cases the minister is given discretionary power to waive the requirement.

2 Preparation

It shall be the duty of the minister, when application is made to him for matrimony to be solemnized, to inquire whether there be any impediment either to the marriage or to the solemnization thereof. It shall also be the duty of the minister to provide or secure appropriate means of education so that all who seek marriage in the Church may

come to it with a Christian understanding of its purpose and may be encouraged to give effect with God's help to the vows which they are preparing to make.

The parties to the intended marriage, after due consideration, shall be encouraged to sign the Declaration set out in Schedule A.

The minister is not required himself to provide the appropriate means of education for marriage; he may secure its provision by others. Many agencies today sponsor education for marriage. The appropriate means will vary from one social pattern to another and from one culture to another, even in our own country. Methods of adult education involving peer groups, dialogue, and the use of resources drawn from various media now supplement, or replace the lecture and one-to-one instruction of earlier days, as more effective means of instruction.

3 Impediments of Kindred or Affinity

In making the inquiries directed in clause 2 above, the minister shall, with respect to the impediments of kindred and affinity, be governed by the following table in which marriages between certain persons are forbidden:

A Man may not marry his	A Woman may not marry her
1 Mother	1 Father
2 Step-mother	2 Step-father
3 Mother-in-law	3 Father-in-law
4 Daughter	4 Son
5 Step-daughter	5 Step-son
6 Daughter-in-law	6 Son-in-law
7 Sister	7 Brother
8 Grandmother	8 Grandfather
9 Grandfather's wife	9 Grandmother's husband
10 Wife's Grandmother	10 Husband's Grandfather

11	Grand-daughter	11	Grandson
12	Wife's Grand-daughter	12	Husband's Grandson
13	Grandson's Wife	13	Grand-daughter's Husband
14	Aunt	14	Uncle
15	Niece	15	Nephew

The absence of impediments can easily be determined in friendly conversation with individual couples, without turning the enquiry into an inquisition. A careful and friendly enquiry, guided by a knowledge of the impediments, will serve to guarantee a legally valid marriage. A sensitive and well-informed practice of pastoral conversation will often be required when confronted with impediments or the suspicion of impediments related to age, consent, concealment, prior contracts, baptism or Christian commitment.

The declaration provided in schedule A is not a redundant rehearsal of the marriage vows; it is a simple promise to prepare for the making of those vows. The declaration requires the use of no theological language nor any declaration of religious faith, so that it may be proposed to an inquirer or to an unbeliever at the outset, and without threat to his integrity, before he has been able even to consider the Christian doctrine of marriage.

The subject of impediments of consanguinity and affinity does not now excite the same interest that it did in the later Middle Ages, or even in the Victorian era. The subject is treated briefly in *Marriage in Church and State* (p. 28) where it is pointed out that the table does not conform in every particular to Canadian legislation. For the social significance of the impediments, the reader is referred to *Kindred and Affinity as Impediments to Marriage*, the report of a commission appointed by the Archbishop of Canterbury (London, 1940) especially appendix 3 by Professor B. Malinowski.

4   Age

No minister shall solemnize the marriage of persons either of whom is under sixteen years of age, except that for sufficient cause and only in accordance with the provisions of the civil law he may do so, provided that he first refer the case to the bishop of the diocese and follow his order and direction, except that a Bishop may give permission to a Priest under his licence to act herein without notice, provided that he report actions under this Section to his Bishop as soon as possible.

The reasons for requiring a higher age for marriage

The church in its Canon law has not hesitated to go beyond the minimum requirements of the civil law to enable it to fulfil Christian purposes. In this instance the church is serving society by leading it away from child marriage, and thus widening the scope of possibility for marriage to be based on consent freely arrived at. There are still a few remote areas among the aboriginal peoples of Canada where bishops may find it necessary to dispense with this rule, but even there the obligation of leadership cannot be abrogated by the church.

5   Requirements of Civil Law

The minister shall assure himself that all the requirements of the civil law of the province or other jurisdiction in which the marriage is to be solemnized have been met, in particular that all prerequisite notices, medical certificates, and consents of parents, guardians, or others, have been respectively given, completed, and obtained.

This clause draws the attention of those who intend to marry, and of pastors, to various important civil requirements. The fulfilment of these obligations can be greatly facilitated if due notice is given as required by clause 1. The fulfillment of these various obligations, which vary somewhat from province to province, provide pastors with many opportunities for education and pastoral care. (cf. *"Marriage in Church and State,"* pp. 28–30.)

6 Banns and Licence to Marry

The minister shall also assure himself that the banns of the persons to be married have been published in the manner required in this Canon and in conformity with the requirements of civil law; or in lieu of such publication, that a licence has been obtained from the proper authority.

7 Publication of Banns

When Banns are to be published,

A They shall be called in the church three several Sundays during divine worship after the accustomed manner, and in conformity with the requirements of civil law,

B Whether either or both of the parties are accustomed to worship in a church or churches other than their own parish church, the banns may be called in the church or churches in which they worship, provided that the civil law allows such procedure,

C The minister shall say together with such addition as the civil law may require: I publish the Banns of Marriage between N. of ... and N. of ... If any of you know cause or just impediment, why these two persons should not be joined together in Holy Matrimony, you are to declare it. This is the first (or second or third) time of asking,

D After the final calling their publication shall be recorded as required, and if the marriage is to be solemnized elsewhere the appropriate certificate shall be forwarded to the officiating minister.

8   When Licence to Marry is Required

The calling of banns shall not exempt the parties from obtaining a licence to marry where the civil law requires them to do so.

Clauses 6–8 gather into one place what is required to be known regarding the publication of banns. It is assumed by the church that banns are to be called whenever possible, even though in some circumstances a civil licence may be required as well, or its acquisition found expedient.

Even when the parties require a licence and are unknown to the congregation, the calling of banns places marriage within the context of the household of God in the Christian congregation, some of whom, the ceremony implies, must surely have obligations toward the couple coming to be married in their parish church.

The earlier parts of this Canon are concerned with normal marriage and its support. Exceptions are dealt with independently later.

9   Certain Marriages Forbidden

Except as provided in Part III or Part IV of this Canon, no minister shall solemnize the marriage of two persons one of whom has been a party to a ceremony of marriage with a third person now living.

10   Baptism

The Form of Solemnization of Matrimony in the Book of Common Prayer is provided for the marriage of Christians. No minister shall solemnize matrimony between two persons neither of whom has been baptized. If two persons, one of whom has not been baptized, desire to be so married, he shall refer the matter to the bishop of the diocese and follow his order and direction.

This clause is for the guidance of pastors confronted with uncertainties arising from some combination of the following circumstances: (a) the Prayer Book service assumes that two Christians are being married, and a rubric on p. 571 contains the assumption that both are communicants; (b) the requirements for civil marriage are felt by some applicants to be sufficient to qualify them for marriage in the church, even though these requirements, naturally enough, do not include either baptism or profession of faith; (c) St Paul in the New Testament, and ultimately the Canon law itself, tended strongly to impose on Christians the duty of finding marriage partners from among their fellow believers. The Canon law of the Episcopal Church in the U.S.A. requires that one party be baptized; the Canon law of the English revision proposed (as here) that if only one party is baptized, the direction of the bishop must be sought and followed. The difficulties are discussed further in *Marriage in Church and State* (pp. 29f).

There seem to be three ways of identifying a Christian, and they are found respectively in (a) ethical-social, (b) religious, and (c) more strictly theological discourse. Thus (a) it may be said of anyone that he is a "good Christian" regardless of his religious profession or even if he admits to none. Then (b) it may be said simply that someone is a Christian, or a practising Christian, implying that he can be identified by some open expression of faith or visible religious practice, generally admirable but sometimes perhaps fanatical. Finally (c) we may recognize that someone is a Christian simply by the fact of his having been made one in baptism, and we do not thereby of necessity raise any question as to the present quality of his life. The first meaning is not relevant to our purpose. The second meaning commends itself readily to our highly moralistic culture, though it would place an impossible burden on a pastor to have to determine how "good" a Christian anyone must be to qualify for marriage in the church. The third meaning has the merit of simplicity — either one has been baptized or not, or one can be conditionally baptized; it also has the merit of a long history in Canon law, and it rests upon the importance of the sign of God's acceptance rather than upon human achievement. The pastor is not asked to sit in judgment on the moral quality of the applicant but to determine his baptismal status; he is free to assist him pastorally in any way that may seem appropriate.

11 Licence and Permission of Minister to Solemnize Marriage

A **Every minister who solemnizes a marriage must, where the civil authorities make such a requirement, hold a valid licence or permit to officiate at marriages in that place.**

B **He must also have the licence or authority of the bishop of the diocese in which the marriage is to be solemnized.**

C **In any parish other than that to which he is licensed the officiating minister must have obtained the consent of the incumbent of the parish in which the marriage is to be solemnized.**

D **The discretion of a minister to decline to solemnize any particular marriage shall not be abrogated by this Canon.**

Clause 11 gathers into one place what must be known concerning certain obligations of the clergy. Failure to understand or observe all of these is productive of much confusion and, on occasion, failure in some particular may lead to the solemnization of a marriage which is irregular and, in a few cases, also invalid in civil law.

Part II
The Solemnization of Matrimony

The Solemnization of Matrimony, in which a bride and groom marry each other by the mutual exchange of solemn promises and vows, is too serious an undertaking not to require every precaution that it should always be carefully performed. Marriages cannot be taken anywhere by anybody, not even by a clergyman. The service should lead to deeper understanding of the meaning of marriage. To this end the elimination of unseemly music and other discordant elements should be assured. When it cannot be avoided that a Christian marries an unbeliever, the unbeliever should not be required to do violence to conscience by the recitation of particular religious formulae which he does not accept. On the other hand, he or she must be required to make the promises and vows required by marriage in the church, if this is what is sincerely desired. There are no provisions for exceptions of any kind at present. With the massive population movements of modern times, provision for exceptional cases becomes urgent. In many parts of the world, even in pockets of British, European, and American society, practising Christians — or even baptized Christians — are a minority. In these circumstances many are likely to form unions with members of the surrounding culture, whatever steps may be recommended to discourage them from doing so.

1   Place of Marriage

Marriage shall be solemnized in the body of the church except for sufficient cause, in the face of the congregation and of the friends and neighbours of those who come to be married. Every marriage shall be solemnized in the presence of at least two witnesses in addition to the officiating minister.

This clause combines a rubrical direction on p. 564 of the Prayer Book with the minimum civil requirement for witnesses at a wedding, and makes the latter expressly part of Canon law.

2   Incumbent in Charge of Service

The incumbent shall be responsible for the conduct of the marriage service. Hymns or anthems sung at the service shall be those only which may be found in Holy Scripture, in the books of Common Prayer or Common Praise, or in texts approved by ecclesiastical authority.

There is a similar provision in a Canon of the Episcopal Church in the U.S.A. It strengthens the hand of hard-pressed incumbents seeking with charity to establish greater dignity at weddings.

3   Marriage to a Non-Christian

When one party to a marriage is an unbeliever, the minister may if he sees fit use the Form of Solemnization of Matrimony with such modifications as may be permitted by the bishop of the diocese where the marriage is to be solemnized; no alteration may be made either in the declaration of intention or in the vow made by the unbeliever except by omission of the words "holy" and "according to God's ordinance."

As Christians are increasingly in a minority position in current population trends, the problem which this provision is designed to meet will become more widespread, and direction with regard to it more urgently needed. The provision is drafted to achieve two ends: respect for the conscience of the unbeliever regarding the use of specifically religious formulae; and assurance that the actual contract of marriage will not be weakened in any particular. Within these limits latitude is given for the exercise of episcopal and pastoral discretion.

4   Parish and Civil Registers

It is the duty of the officiating minister to record the information required by the civil authority as well as the infor-

mation necessary for pastoral care, in the manner following:

A   At the time of marriage the minister shall enter the several particulars relating thereto in a register to be retained in the parish for this purpose. In this parish register he shall record the particulars required by the civil law; he shall also record the particulars of baptism, confirmation, and church membership of the respective parties, and the address of their intended residence.

B   The minister shall also record in such other register or form as may be required by the civil law the particulars prescribed by that law, and shall duly report the same to the appropriate authority.

This clause has been drafted so that it will not conflict with the provision of any civil jurisdiction in Canada. It has been designed to assure that in every church there shall be a register which shows not only the facts required by civil law, but facts required to be known in the course of parish administration and pastoral work, in particular the ecclesiastical status of the parties and their intended residence — these last being especially important if transfer to another parish is contemplated.

General Introduction to Parts III–VII

Relation of these to the Earlier Parts of the Canon

The word *marriage* has at least four meanings which must be carefully distinguished, for all are in common use and all appear in the Canon:

a   Marriage is a union or status in which two persons are bound together by legal ties which may also include religious ones. The qualities of this union vary, but those to which Christians should aim to commit themselves are described in the opening sentence of the preface and are again referred to in Part III, 1(A). It is characteristic of the union or status of marriage that one may inquire how long it lasted — for life, or for so many years. The breakdown of this union and the desire to form another constitute the whole subject matter of Part IV;

b Marriage also denotes a contract. The Christian criteria of this contract are described in the second sentence of the preface; it is also the principal subject matter of all but the last clause of Part III of the Canon. It is characteristic of the contract that one may inquire whether the parties were competent to make it, what they contracted to do, whether they did so in proper form, and when they did it;

c Mariage refers also to an institution of human society, as when we speak of African marriage or Levirate marriage; however, expressions like these may sometimes be closely related to family. The third sentence of the preface describes our present understanding of the purposes of marriage which distinguish it as a Christian institution constitutive of the family. These purposes figure prominently in the liturgy of marriage. Their absence may vitiate the contract (Part III, 2(B)) or may cause the union to break down;

d The word marriage is also commonly used of the ceremony of marriage; but this usage is hardly to be distinguished from the contract of which the ceremony is the context and outward form, certifying as far as may be that the contract was in fact undertaken. Part III also deals with defects in the ceremony for they are inextricably related to the contract. The ceremony is said to be solemnized by the officiant, but the contract is made by the bride and groom who marry each other.

43

Choices before the Pastor

First, the pastor should have some sociological understanding of the actual institutions of marriage which prevail in his or her parish, and the strains to which they are subject in a changing and pluralistic society. He or she and the congregation should be able to bring to these institutions, through pastoral care, the strength and clarity of purpose that are claimed for the Christian institution of marriage.

Secondly, the pastor is responsible for seeing that the contract of marriage is understood and properly made in each case. For this, premarital preparation is required in a manner consonant with the culture in which it is offered.

Thirdly, the pastor is responsible for giving leadership to his or her community, in the provision of pastoral care where it may be needed for those who, having entered the status of marriage, find it threatened beyond their ability to manage, or broken down beyond a reasonable possibility of reconciliation.

This threefold task is implied or described in the earlier parts of the Canon. Where the breakdown of a supposed marriage appears to be related to the inadequacy of the contract with which it began, the pastor may look to Part III for a remedy. If this breakdown of the marriage appears to have developed *after* it was validly contracted, he or she may look to Part IV for a remedy, though only for a spouse who (after civil divorce) seeks to marry again during the lifetime of a former partner. If the pastor encounters one who seeks communicant status through baptism, confirmation, or admission to communion, and whose marital status is in doubt according to this Canon, he or she may seek a remedy through Part V. These cases all represent exceptions, and they may indicate the extent to which individual or social defects have not been remedied by the pastoral measures proposed in the preface and Parts I and II, where the most urgent tasks of the church in relation to marriage are described.

The Problem of "Indissolubility"

In its most highly developed form, western Canon law came eventually to establish approximately the following conditions for a valid and indissoluble Christian marriage: (a) it must be between two baptized Christians; (b) they must both be legally competent to marry by age, status, etc. (a provision which accounts among other things for the practice of posting of the "Table of Kindred and Affinity" in the church porch); (c) they must freely exchange vows of life-long fidelity and not merely fidelity for a trial period or to satisfy someone else; (d) they must intend the purpose of marriage which includes mutual fellowship and the pro-creation (if it may be) of children; (e) they must do all this in the manner prescribed from time to time by Canon law (now usually in the presence of two witnesses and an authorized minister); and (f) after the contract has been made they must consummate the marriage before its validity to become established.

If all these conditions have been met, then, according to the developed Canon law of the West, such a marriage cannot be dissolved by any human authority. It can only be dissolved by death. This doctrine had two notable consequences among others, one good and one bad. The less desirable consequence, which we shall mention first, was not a necessary one, however likely its occurrence may seem to some observers.

In the later Middle Ages, when a marriage broke down, or when a man wanted to marry somebody else, as in the case of Henry VIII, there developed a widespread practice of looking for any reason that could be found, trivial or otherwise, for alleging that one of the conditions prescribed for valid marriage at the time had not been met. The method differed morally in no essential way from the modern practice, in some jurisdictions, of alleging trivial reasons for divorce. However, the proliferation of far-reaching grounds of nullity at this period precluded the necessity of seeking dissolution in many cases of marital breakdown. Fears sometimes expressed of the present Roman Catholic doctrine of indissolubility rest on the judgment, of those who express them, that the Roman Church's theory of nullity is still too broad. Not all Anglicans, however, would concur in this judgment, nor in a like judgment that the Canon law of the Episcopal Church in the U.S.A. suffers from a similar weakness.

No one however now doubts the corruption of the Canon law in the later Middle Ages. The reformers reacted against this corruption with such violence that their followers have sometimes tended to err in the opposite direction and so to find themselves with no ecclesiastical marriage law at all, or else with one that is too vague or too brief to offer much specific guidance in difficult cases. The "Table of Kindred and Affinity" which adorns church porches to this day was in part the result of a common sense move to get rid of the deviously devised tables of an earlier period. We should certainly sympathize with the reformers, and no one today can reasonably quarrel with this aspect of their work.

The last point introduces us to the good result of the tradition of the western Canon law. This has been to make people take very seriously the preparation for a union of such firm character. It is owing to this tradition that, in the marriage service, we have so many reminders that marriage must not be undertaken lightly, nor undertaken in defiance of any (legal) cause or just impediment, which might make the marriage unlawful and, therefore, not a marriage in the sight of God according to the conditions laid down in the Canons. Obviously, nobody can know for certain what in every instance may be exactly true or not true in the sight of God, but the church has the duty as "a witness and a keeper of holy writ" to interpret scripture on this subject in accordance with the best knowledge available at the time and in reliance on the guidance of the Spirit. The Canon law based on this interpretation governs

46

external actions and, like other human law, cannot always be binding in conscience.

Over the years, and especially since the Reformation, canonists have taken many steps to remedy the defects of the earlier tradition, and so to prevent merely trivial grounds of nullity being alleged. The reaction has gone very far under the influence of the civil law, so that now it is difficult in some cases in some jurisdictions to get a marriage declared null at all. This is one reason why lawyers sometimes feel obliged to recommend to their clients that they will be more likely to terminate their purported marriage by a suit for divorce rather than by one for nullity, if grounds can also be found for the former. In these circumstances the Canon law would seem to some to be on the side of common sense. At all events, the practical result of this particular approach to broken marriages can hardly be better expressed than in the words of Chancellor H.B. Vaisey (later Sir Harry Vaisey, judge of the High Court in England), which are included in an appendix to the report presented in 1935 to the Convocations of Canterbury and York.

When a marriage, or supposed marriage, has come to shipwreck and the parties are separated without hope of reconciliation, it is surely permissible to scrutinize the conditions and circumstances of the case with the utmost care, to see whether by any chance a union so unblessed was ever a marriage at all — whether, in other words, there has not all along been a way of escape for the parties from their bond, and one, moreover, which does not involve any derogation from the principles upon which marriage is founded. Difficult though the identification of such cases may be, the church should not shrink from denying the reality of a marriage or a union formed irregularly in any of those points which it now recognizes, or may hereafter be prepared to recognize, as essential and vital; nor should

47

there be hesitation in treating as null the marriage of persons whom the state has divorced on grounds or circumstances which would have justified those persons in proceeding for nullity.

Part III
Determination of Marital Status Under this Canon

The pastor should note that three classes of person may be given relief under Part III (clauses 3, 4, and 6):

a   Those whose former marriage or purported marriage has been civilly annulled or declared null and void, and who desire a ruling from the church that their former union "did not result in marrige under the Canon and therefore does not constitute an impediment to marriage" in this church. (This ruling may be sought whether or not the applicant desires to marry after receiving a decision);

b   Those whose former marriage or purported marriage has been terminated by civil divorce and who seeks the same ruling as above in the same circumstances. (i.e. Those who seek the church's declaration of nullity);

c   Those whose former spouse presumed dead and who seek a new marriage in the church.

Many Christians, wishing to uphold the tradition of the Canon law of western Christendom, will wish and should be encouraged to seek relief under (b) above instead of under the provision of Part IV. Because of differences between civil and canonical legislation, this may often be possible as Part III, 2 may indicate.

An applicant under this part who is not currently intending to marry must apply through his own parish priest. One who is intending to marry must apply through the incumbent where he or she proposes to seek the marriage rites.

1 Definitions

A "Marriage" as defined by this Canon means that union described in the Preface of this Canon and further described in clause 2 of this Part. With respect to marriage so defined, a man and a woman may nevertheless, for reasons of age or health or other serious cause agree to marry upon condition that there shall be no sexual intercourse between them permanently or for a limited time or from time to time.

B "Commission" as used in this Canon means the Ecclesiastical Matrimonial Commission established under Part VI of this Canon, and the effect of a decision of a Commission shall be as stated in clause 6 of Part VI.

In defining marriage by reference to the preface and clause 2, this clause frees the church's matrimonial discipline from complete indentification with the civil institution of marriage, which is now hardly even nominally Christian. The definition of commission ties this Part in with Part VI.

2 Conditions of Valid Marriage under this Canon

The question whether a purported marriage constitued a marriage as defined by this Canon shall be determined by the Commission in accordance with the following principles:

A The parties to a marriage are not qualified for the purpose of this Canon to marry each other if —

  1 Either of them is under the age of 16 years, except as provided in clause 4 of Part I of this Canon,

  2 They are related to each other by blood or marriage within the prohibited degrees listed in the Table of Kindred and Affinity set out in clause 3 of Part I of this Canon,

3   Either of them has gone through a ceremony of marriage with a person who is living at the time of the application, unless

   a   The previous ceremony of marriage has been found, as provided in this Part, by the Commission not to have been a marriage as defined by this Canon and therefore not to be an impediment to marriage under the Canon Law of this Church, or

   b   The previous marriage has been found by the Commission to have been dissolved or terminated according to the civil law applicable thereto and permission to marry has been given by the Commission, as provided by Part IV of this Canon.

B   The contract of marriage requires the free and voluntary consent of the parties to marry each other upon the terms set out in the Preface of this Canon, based upon adequate understanding by each of them of the nature of the union and of the mutual relations of husband and wife and of parents and children.

C   Consent to marry is not present where —

   1   One of the parties is at the time of the contract of marriage incapable by reason of mental defect, mental illness, alcoholic intoxication, or the influence of a drug, of having the necessary understanding or giving the necessary consent,

   2   One of the parties has been induced to consent by duress, by coercion, or by fear,

   3   The woman gives consent after having been abducted and before being set free,

   4   One of the parties is at the time of the contract of marriage mistaken with respect to the nature of the contract or of the union, or with respect to the identity of the other party,

5   One of the parties is at the time of the contract of marriage deceived by misrepresentation or concealment of facts seriously detrimental to the establishment of the contract, including among other things misrepresentation or concealment of

  a Venereal disease,

  b Addiction to drugs or alcohol,

  c Pregnancy, except as a result of intercourse with the man,

  d Addiction to homosexual practice, sadistic conduct, or other abnormal practice endangering the life or health of the other party,

6   The marriage has been agreed to upon a condition which is illegal, impossible or contrary to the nature of the union, as defined in this Canon,

7   The marriage is intended to be a sham or mere form,

8   Either party is incapable of consummating or unreasonably refuses to consummate the marriage by sexual intercourse, subject to clause 1 (A) of this Part,

9   One of the parties is not a Christian and there is a condition that the Christian party shall be entitled to adhere to and practise Christianity or to bring up any children of the union as Christians, and the non-Christian party assents to the condition without intending that it shall be satisfied.

D In the cases mentioned in sub-paragraphs (2)(3)(4) (5) and (9) hereof, the party coerced, mistaken or deceived or otherwise imposed upon may by an act of will approbate the marriage and continue to cohabit with the other party when free to cease cohabitation after being freed from coercion, fear or abduction or after learning of the mistake,

deception, concealment or other circumstance constituting the defect. What constitutes approbation is a question of fact in each case. The effect of approbation for the purpose of this Canon is to validate the marriage.

E **Nothing contained in this Canon shall authorize the solemnization of a marriage known to the minister or either of the parties to be invalid by civil law.**

The conditions of valid marriage under this Canon are designed to set out the church's specific definition, in terms of Canon law, of marriage as defined doctrinally in Part I. They are based on a study of the Canons of the Church of England, the Anglican Church of Canada, the Protestant Episcopal Church in the U.S.A. as well as the civil laws of England, the common law provinces of Canada, Quebec, and certain jurisdictions in the U.S.A.

The distinctive characteristics of the code here set out, which the commission recommends as improvements over the civil laws of any of the countries and jurisdictions concerned, and in some measure over any of the Canon laws studied, are as follows.

a   The minimum age of 16, corresponding to the present English minimum but with provision for exception for grave cause (see *Marriage in Church and State*, pp. 28f.);

b   Rejection of sham marriages. Here, the civil laws of England and our common law provinces are particularly defective;

c   Recognition of the effect of certain conditions as rendering true marriage impossible;

d   Clarification of the doctrine of approbation;

e   Avoidance of loose employment of the language of nullity to conceal widely discretionary power to allow remarriage of divorced persons.

3 Conditions Governing Application regarding Canonical Status

A   An application for declaration of marital status under this Canon may be made where the applicant has gone through a ceremony of marriage with a person living at the time of the application and it is alleged that the ceremony did not constitute a marriage as defined by this Canon and where the marriage or purported marriage

1   Has been annulled or declared null and void or dissolved or otherwise terminated by a legislature or court, or

2   Is alleged to have been dissolved or otherwise terminated according to the civil law properly applicable thereto, by an extra-judicial or non-judicial and non-legislative act or event.

B   An application under this clause may be made by a person who has gone through a ceremony mentioned in sub-clause (A) of this clause and who is

1   A member of this Church, or

2   A person who desires to marry according to the rites of this Church.

C   1   An application under this clause not made in the course of or with a view to proceedings preliminary to a marriage shall be made to the incumbent of the parish or mission where the applicant resides or is accustomed to worship.

2   An application under this clause made in the course of or with a view to proceedings preliminary to a marriage shall be made to the incumbent of the parish or mission where it is desired that the intended marriage be celebrated.

3   The incumbent receiving the application shall investigate it to the best of his ability and forward the

application, together with his report thereon, through the appropriate channels to the Commission having jurisdiction in the diocese.

Application for declaration of marital status under the Canon may be made by a member of the church who wishes merely to have his or her status determined for the sake of his or her conscience or by a person, whether a member of the church or not, who wishes to marry according to the rites of the church. The church must offer its ministry of marriage to all who wish to receive it, and not only to its own members, but clause 10 of Part II requires that at least one of the parties to a marriage celebrated according to its rites must have been baptized.

Application may be made not only when a ceremony of marriage entered into by the applicant has been civilly annulled or declared null and void, but also where it has been dissolved by a civil authority by legislative, judicial, or extra-judicial divorce.

In case of doubt, the commission may require the applicant to obtain a declaration respecting the validity of the marriage or of the dissolution from a civil court.

4   Form of Application

A   **An application for declaration of marital status under clause 3 shall be made in writing and signed by the applicant and shall contain the information required by Schedule B.**

B   **The application shall be accompanied by —**

   1   A certificate of performance or registration of the ceremony issued by a competent authority,

   2   The original or a copy of the legislative act or the judgment or decree referred to in Schedule B paragraphs 9 and 10, and of any other document necessary for proof of any fact, and proof of its authenticity,

3   Statements in writing verifying all other relevant facts not within the knowledge of the applicant signed by persons having knowledge of the facts,

4   Where there has been no legislative act and no judgment or decree as above mentioned, a reasoned opinion in writing, signed by a person professionally qualified to give an opinion in respect of the law in question, verifying that the purported marriage has been dissolved or otherwise terminated.

In the formal and substantial requirements for the application, attention is drawn to the concern of the church for the welfare of children of the union now being questioned, and facts relating to the custody, maintenance, and education of dependent children are required. The welfare of the other party to the union is also of concern, and it must be shown how he or she is being maintained, and if not by the applicant an explanation is required.

The other information is demanded to enable the commission to determine the validity of the ceremony under the Canon and to ascertain for its own purposes the civil status of the union.

5   Decision of Commission

On an application for declaration of marital status under clause 3 of this Part, the Commission, when all relevant facts have been proved to its satisfaction, shall determine whether the ceremony gone through by the applicant resulted in a marriage under this Canon. If the Commission determines that the ceremony did not result in a marriage under this Canon and if the Commission is satisfied that the marriage or purported marriage has been annulled or declared null and void or dissolved or otherwise terminated by a legislature or competent court, or has been dissolved or otherwise terminated by another act or event according to the law properly applicable thereto, and that no civil impediment to the marriage of the applicant exists, the Commission shall make a declaration that the ceremony in question did not result in a marriage under this Canon and therefore does not constitute an impediment to marriage under the Canon Law of this Church. In all other cases, the Commission shall declare that impediment exists.

Where there has been a failure to obtain any consent of a parent, guardian or other person, other than a party to the marriage, whose consent is required by the applicable civil law and where the marriage has been annulled on this ground by a competent court, the Commission may make a declaration that the ceremony in question did not result in a marriage under this Canon and therefore does not constitute an impediment to marriage under the Canon Law of this Church.

If the ceremony in question is found to have resulted in a marriage as defined by the Canon, the commission will declare that an impediment to remarriage of the applicant exists. If the ceremony is found not to have resulted in a marriage as defined by the Canon;

a impediment will nevertheless exist if the commission finds for its purpose that the ceremony resulted in a valid civil marriage that has not been civilly terminated by divorce; or

b if the commission finds for its purpose that it did not result in a valid civil marriage or that it has been terminated by civil dissolution, the commission will declare that the ceremony does not constitute an impediment to remarriage under the Canon.

Annulments for grounds not recognized as canonical under this Part are treated as dissolutions.

6 Presumption of Death

A) An application for declaration of marital status under this Canon may be made to the Commission by a person who desires to be married according to the rites of this Church and who has been a party to a marriage with a person

1 In respect of whom a judicial declaration of presumption of death has been made by a competent court, or

2 Who is missing and presumed dead but whose death has not been officially confirmed and in respect of whom no judicial declaration of presumption of death mentioned in sub-paragraph (1) has been made.

B For the purpose of the application a court exercising civil jurisdiction in any part of Canada acting under legislation of Canada or of a province is deemed to be a competent court, whether the declaration is made under legislation related to marriage or under other legislation. The jurisdiction of any other court whose declaration is relied on must be proved to the satisfaction of the Commission.

C The application shall be made in accordance with the provisions of clause 3 paragraph C (2) and (3) and Schedule B omitting paragraphs 3 to 8 inclusive.

D The application shall be accompanied by a certified copy of the judicial declaration, if any, relied on by the applicant, a statement or statements in writing signed by the person or persons having knowledge of the facts on which the allegation of death is based, and a statement in writing signed by the applicant setting out his or her belief in the death of the other party to the marriage and the reasons for that belief.

E   If the Commission is satisfied that the missing party to the marriage or ceremony of marriage is dead, as far as can be ascertained at the time of the application, the Commission may make a finding to that effect and make a declaration that the marriage or ceremony of marriage between the applicant and the missing party does not at the time of the declaration constitute an impediment to the marriage of the applicant under the Canon Law of this Church. Otherwise, the Commission shall dismiss the application without prejudice to a later application.

F   A person who has obtained a declaration under this clause shall at or after the time of publication of banns or on production of the licence declare to the intended celebrant that he or she has no reason to believe and does not believe that the other party to the former marriage or ceremony of marriage is alive.

The civil laws in Canada are defective in providing no adequate machinery for declaration of presumption of death. Proceedings under some provincial marriage legislation lead only to the issue of a licence to remarry; the applicant must acknowledge that a remarriage will be void if the missing spouse is in fact alive and has not validly terminated the marriage. The church might well urge that the Parliament of Canada should enact proper legislation, but in the meantime clause 6 offers relief under the church's discipline for spouses who are "neither married nor widowed" if they can satisfy the commission that the missing partner is dead, as far as can be ascertained at the time of the application.

Part IV
The Remarriage of a Divorced Person Whose Former Spouse is Living

Introduction
Remarriage after Divorce

Those who have renewed the church's Canon on marriage argue that the proper interpretation of the teaching of Christ applicable to our own day is that, while the marriage bond ought to be held in the highest esteem and everything possible done to maintain it, it can nevertheless be broken by human authority for grave cause. Where a civil divorce has been granted, the church should be free, through a duly authorized ecclesiastical body, to grant permission to such a persion to be married in the church. On this view, therefore, part of the solution for certain broken marriages is sought in civil divorce, and the chief problem for Christians as members of civil society is the development by the state of a just divorce law. The proponents of this view rely heavily on the action of civil courts and, therefore, must accept responsibility for working toward the reform of divorce legislation.

The proponents of the present western canonical tradition are aware that the doctrine of the indissolubility of marriage has never been universally accepted throughout Christendom; the doctrine and the Canon law depending upon it developed and spread gradually in the West, though indissolubility was firmly established as the rule before the twelfth century, subject to narrowly limited exceptions, each case requiring papal permission for remarriage. Moreover the Eastern Orthodox churches grant divorce with the right of remarriage, claiming the discipline to rest upon the gospel. This fact must be noted despite western distaste for certain peculiarities of eastern thought, and despite the Greek church's evident dependence in early days upon civil codes.

In New Testament times divorce was evidently sometimes justified on one of two grounds then recognized in the church: adultery (Matt 5:32); and the desertion of a Christian husband or wife by his or her pagan partner (1 Cor 7:15).

Today two questions arise: (a) after such a divorce has either partner the right to remarry while their former spouse is still living; (b) are there other grounds justifying divorce besides the two that happen to be mentioned in the New Testament? To the latter question we answer, yes, without hesitation. There are many worse things than adultery and desertion justifying divorce. To the question of whether civil divorce granted to a Christian gives the right to remarry in the church during the lifetime of a former sposue, we must reply with all due caution: sometimes.

We cannot believe that the two particular exceptions mentioned in the New Testament exhaust the possibilities for the relief of an especially poignant form of suffering. However difficult the task, a Canon must make some provision for these and other cases, though the provision must be expressly for the purposes of the church in the care of its members, or of those who seek the church's care, and not for the purpose of performing any function of a civil court or other civil authority.

We believe that this general approach may be construed as our recommendation for some part of the response which should be made to resolution 95 of the 1984 Lambeth Conference which reads as follows.

Mindful of the needs of those who are in deep distress and claim the Church's sympathy, the Conference urges that Provincial and regional churches should consider how best their pastoral responsibility towards those who do not conform to our Lord's standard can be discharged.

The conference declined itself to make any authoritative judgment on this point, and laid the burden on the constituent members of the Anglican communion.

1 Application for Permission to Remarry according to the Rites of the Church

A An application for permission to marry each other according to the rites of this Church may be made by two persons, one or both of whom has or have gone through a ceremony or ceremonies of marriage with a person or persons now living not a party or parties to the application, if the prior marriage or marriages is or are not questioned under this Canon in the application but has or have been dissolved or terminated by a legislature or legislatures or a court or courts or by another act or acts or event or events according to the law or laws applicable thereto. Where a marriage or purported marriage has been annulled for a defect not mentioned in clause 2 of Part III of this Canon, and no defect mentioned in that clause is alleged in respect thereof, it shall be deemed for the purposes of this Canon to have been dissolved.

B The application shall be made to the incumbent of the parish or mission where it is desired that the intended marriage be celebrated. The incumbent shall investigate the application to the best of his ability and forward it together with his report thereon, through the appropriate channels, to the Ecclesiastical Matrimonial Commission established under Part VI of this Canon having jurisdiction in the diocese.

C The application shall be made in writing and signed by both applicants and shall contain the information required by Schedule C.

Under this clause, an application for permission to marry according to the rites of the church is made by both parties to the intended marriage when either or both has or have been divorced from a union or unions resulting in marriage as defined by the Canon and the former partner or partners is or are living. Neither party need be a member of the Anglican church, but at least one must have been baptized.

Persons whose former unions have been annulled for defects not recognized in Part III may apply for permission under this Part.

Formal requirements are intended to bring forward the considerable body of information the commission must have for its decision. On this point, we have already referred in chapter 2 to the need for uniform procedure in all commissions to avoid the confusion which results from lack of uniform provision.

2 Permission to Remarry according to the Rites of the Church

Permission to marry according to the rites of this Church may be granted by the Commission to the applicants notwithstanding the marriage or marriages of either or both of them to another person or persons now living, if the Commission is satisfied that —

A   Any prior marriage in question has been validly dissolved or terminated in accordance with the law properly applicable thereto,

B   The causes which led to the dissolution or termination were sufficiently grave to justify application under this Part,

C   The applicant concerned tried in good faith before dissolution to effect reconciliation with the other party,

D   If prior marriages of both applicants have been dissolved, there are grounds for special assurance of the probable stability of the intended marriage,

E   There is good reason for permitting the marriage other than an intention to enter into a mere pro forma marriage to legitimate a child or children,

F   If a former wife of the male applicant is living, adequate provision has been made according to his means for the former wife, or there is good reason why the applicant should not be required to make that provision,

G   Proper provision has been made for the care, maintenance, education and advancement of minor, disabled or otherwise dependent children of any prior marriage,

H   If the children of a prior marriage are to live with the applicants, there is a reasonable prospect that the family relationship will be satisfactory,

I   The applicants understand the Christian Doctrine of marriage as defined in this Canon, and intend to enter into such a marriage, and believe on reasonable grounds that they have the capacity to enter into and sustain the marriage during their joint lives.

In accordance with the conclusions of the commission that the legal grounds for divorce are often irrelevant to the true cause of breakdown of the marriage, and that it is not possible to prejudge what may be justification for dissolution of a particular marriage, the conditions for granting permission to remarry are not related to any specific legal grounds for dissolution. The commission is required to be satisfied that the cause of dissolution was sufficiently grave to justify the application, and that the applicant attempted to effect reconciliation before dissolution if it was possible to do so. Proper provision for the former partner and for dependent children is a prerequisite to approval. If the children are to live with the applicant, it must be shown that the family relationship is likely to be satisfactory.

The applicants must satisfy the commission that they intend to enter into a Christian marriage as defined by the Canon and that they probably can do so and can sustain the marriage during their joint lives.

The essential points to be established are that the prior marriage was dissolved for no light or insufficient cause and without impetuous or irresponsible haste; that the applicants now genuinely intend to enter into a new union which will, God willing, be and continue to be a Christian marriage for their joint lives; and that they satisfy the commission that they can do so in all probability. In these inquiries there can be no hope of attaining absolute certainty. Men and women in everyday life, and judges and juries in court, daily make decisions based on the evidence available and on probable consequences. The commissions are required by these provisions to make their decisions, based on such probabilities.

Special cases are dealt with here and in clause 4. Where both applicants have been divorced or where either has been divorced more than once, permission will not be granted unless special cause is shown.

3   Refusal of Permission

If permission is not granted, the Commission, subject to clause 4 (C) of this Part, shall dismiss the application which may not be renewed thereafter before any Commission unless further information is available.

If permission is not granted, the application may not be renewed before any commission unless further information is available. Applicants may not shop around for favourable decisions.

4   Special Cases

A   If the Commission is satisfied that efforts towards reconciliation between the parties to a former marriage would have been ineffective as a result of the fault of either party or for any other reason, the requirement of clause 2(C) may be dispensed with.

B   If either applicant has entered into two or more marriages that have been dissolved, the Commission shall not grant permission unless special circumstances justifying permission are proved.

C   Notwithstanding the form of the application, if the Commission is of the opinion that a prior purported marriage of an applicant did not constitute a marriage as defined by this Canon, and the conditions of Part III, clause 5 are satisfied, the Commission may make a declaration under that clause in respect of the marriage in question.

D   If the incumbent of a parish declines for reasons of conscience to solemnize the marriage of a parishioner in his parish pursuant to permission given under this Part, the Bishop shall permit the marriage to be solemnized in a church to be designated by him after consultation with the incumbent in charge.

An application may be made in error under this Part where it should have been made under Part V. In that case, the commission may deal with it under Part V.

Part V
Admission to Holy Communion in Special Cases

In every case where a person who has been remarried, except as provided above in this Canon, whose former and present partners are both living, desires a ruling with respect to admission to Holy Communion, the case must be referred by the incumbent to the bishop of the diocese for his judgment. In arriving at his judgment the bishop shall have due regard for the spiritual welfare of the petitioner as well as the provisions of this Canon. The bishop shall give his judgment in writing to both the incumbent and the petitioner.

This part directs that when certain judgments are requested regarding communicant status, the requests are to be referred to the bishop and his judgment sought. The provision is designed for the guidance of conscience of married persons and their pastors in the circumstances described. It requires no action of the commission and affords no ground for the excommunication of any person for any cause not already set forth in the rubric on page 66 of the Prayer Book. For further discussion, consult *Marriage in Church and State*, pp. 38f.

Part VI
Ecclesiastical Matrimonial Commission

There is a difference between the procedures in the civil court stemming from the common law tradition and those contemplated in the Ecclesiastical Matrimonial Commission.

The pastor should assure an applicant under either Part III or IV that nothing in the Canon justifies or even invites the Ecclesiastical Commission to re-try a case or to initiate any adversary procedures. All that the commission must know about the civil proceedings is simply what they were and their results — facts which, when they have been procured and interpreted by a lawyer, will enable the commission to determine whether the applicant is free to marry under civil law in the parish concerned. The commission passes no judgment on the findings of the civil court and itself has no list of offences which either agree or disagree with those relied upon by the civil authority.

The Commission must be satisfied that the previous marriage has in fact broken down. Beyond this it seeks assurance that the applicant is now behaving responsibly toward existing children or a former spouse. Lastly, it must be convinced by satisfactory evidence as to the serious intention of the couple who now propose to enter upon a new marriage.

1   Diocesan Commission

A   Subject to the provision of clause 2 of this Part, there shall be in each diocese an Ecclesiastical Matrimonial Commission, hereinafter called the Commission, to deal with applications under this Canon.

B   The president of the Commission shall be the diocesan bishop or a bishop or priest appointed by him. In a diocese in which no other president has been appointed, in the absence of the diocesan bishop from the diocese or during a vacancy of the see the administrator of the diocese shall be the president.

C   The diocesan bishop shall appoint two or more communicant members of this Church, clerical or lay, male or female, to be members of the Commission, and may appoint other persons to be consultants without vote.

D   At least one member of the Commission or a consultant should be engaged in or be qualified to engage in the practice or teaching of civil law in the province, territory or other jurisdiction or each of them, in which the Commission acts and at least one member or a consultant should have special skill and knowledge in canon law and at least one in pastoral care.

E   The Commission may delegate to one or more members or consultants the investigation of any application or class of applications and of any matter or matters related thereto and of ascertaining any relevant facts and reporting thereon to the Commission, and may accept an act on any report or may take or require further investigation.

F   The decision of a Commission in respect of an application shall be that of a majority of its members.

G   Before becoming effective, the decision of the Commission shall require confirmation by the diocesan bishop or a bishop appointed by him for the purpose or, if the See is vacant, the metropolitan or a bishop appointed by him for the purpose.

H   The diocesan bishop shall appoint an officer of the Commission who shall be known as the registrar and shall act as clerk and secretary of the Commission, to receive applications, conduct correspondence, give notices, attend hearings and deliberations in person or by deputy and keep minutes of proceedings, and engross and promulgate decisions and communicate each decision to the appropriate incumbent and the applicant or applicants and shall keep the records of the Commission in the diocesan offices.

The diocesan bishop must create a commission under this Part or enter into formation of a joint commission under clause 2. The Diocesan Commission consists of a president who will be the diocesan bishop, unless he appoints a bishop or priest in his place. He will in any event appoint at least two other members who may be clergy or laymen or laywomen, and may appoint assessors as well. At least one of the members or assessors must be qualified in the civil law or laws applicable within the diocese, and one in Canon law and one in pastoral care. One member or assessor may investigate applications and report to the commission which may act on the report or make further investigation.

The role of the commission is to relieve the bishop of the necessity of investigating each application himself, to prepare the required finding and draft a decision for confirmation, and to assist him with advice given by the specially qualified members or assessors.

A majority of the commission must concur in its decisions which must be confirmed by the diocesan bishop or a bishop designated by him. Provision is made for vacancy of the see. The final decision must, therefore, be that of the diocesan bishop unless he delegates the power of confirmation to another bishop.

2 Joint Commission

A **With the consent of the metropolitan of the ecclesiastical province and of the diocesan synods of the dioceses concerned, the diocesan bishops of two or more dioceses may establish a Joint Commission to deal with all applications made thereafter within any of the dioceses concerned. If the dioceses are in different ecclesiastical provinces, the consent of the metropolitan of each province shall be required.**

B **The diocesan bishops of the dioceses concerned shall at the time of the meeting of each provincial synod involved or otherwise from time to time as required elect a bishop to be president of the Joint Commission or confirm the appointment of one already in office. If the jurisdiction of the Joint Commission extends into two ecclesiastical provinces, the bishops of the dioceses concerned shall arrange the election of a president among themselves.**

D **The president of a Joint Commission shall appoint the registrar from time to time during his term of office as president.**

D While a Joint Commission is in existence, its composition, organization, powers and procedure shall with all necessary changes be the same as those of a diocesan Commission, and no diocesan Commission within its jurisdiction shall act, provided that —

1 The diocesan bishops of the dioceses concerned shall join in the appointment of members of and consultants to the Joint Commission,

2 Applications shall be submitted by the appropriate incumbent to the diocesan secretary of each diocese concerned and forwarded by him to the registrar forthwith,

3 After a decision in an application has been made and promulgated, the registrar shall forward the decision, together with the application and all related documents, to the diocesan secretary of the diocese in which it was made, who shall submit the decision for confirmation to the authority mentioned in clause 1(G) of this Part. On obtaining the determination of that authority the secretary shall keep it with the application and accompanying documents in the diocesan records in a confidential manner, and communicate the decision to the appropriate incumbent and the applicant or applicants.

E The diocesan bishop of a diocese under a Joint Commission may with the consent of his diocesan synod and of the metropolitan of the province withdraw his diocese from the jurisdiction of the Joint Commission in respect of applications made after the withdrawal. On so doing he shall forthwith establish a diocesan Commission.

A joint commission may, by consent of the diocesans and synods and the metropolitan or metropolitans, be created for two or more dioceses. Provision is made for appointment of members and a registrar, and for communication with the registrar through diocesan secretaries. On withdrawal of a diocese from such a commission, a Diocesan Commission must be set up in the severed diocese.

Jurisdiction of Commission

Applications under this Canon shall be either

A Applications for declaration of marital status, under Part III of this Canon, or

B Applications for permission to marry according to the rites of this Church, under Part IV of this Canon.

The jurisdiction of the Commission is defined as dealing with applications under Part III or Part IV.

4 Procedure

The procedure followed by a Commission shall be governed by the provisions of Schedule D.

5 Avoidance of Delay

Each application shall be dealt with as expeditiously as possible.

The commission is given broad procedural powers in order that it may function expeditiously, smoothly, efficiently, and inexpensively. It may, but need not, hold hearings. Except in unusual cases, the work of the commission will be to deal with written applications. It is to be anticipated that the commission will rarely find it necessary to hold a hearing. It will likewise be rarely, if ever, necessary for applicants to employ a solicitor or counsel, but the Canon makes provision for applicants to do so if they wish, in order that they may be satisfied that everything that should be said or done on their behalf has been presented to the commission. The normal practice will be that advice of a clergyman will be sufficient. Occasionally, his further assistance will be required.

A declaration of a civil court may be required. Persons involved may be represented by experts in Canon law or pastoral care, or by counsel as mentioned above, or they may act for themselves.

Applications may be reopened only if fresh information is available.

Limitation of Jurisdiction

Every finding and determination of the Commission shall be and shall be expressly stated to be made solely for the purposes of this Canon and not for the purpose of performing any function of a civil court or other civil authority, and shall otherwise be confined to the findings and declaration, or granting or refusal of permission, necessary for disposing of the application in respect of which it is made.

It is expressly required that the commission acknowledge in each case that it is not competing with civil courts or other civil authorities, and that its findings and determinations have no effect in civil law.

Note — Applications to the commission must be made through the incumbent of a parish. See Part V, Clause 3(c), and Part VI, Clause 1(b). Where the application is for permission to marry or is made in the course of, or with a view to, proceedings preliminary to marriage, it is made through the incumbent of the parish where it is desired that the intended marriage be celebrated. Otherwise, it is made through the incumbent of the parish where the applicant resides or is accustomed to worship.

7 Persons Serving in or Attached to the Canadian Armed Forces

A **This section applies to a person enrolled in the Canadian Forces who is serving in the regular forces or** who is a member of the reserve force on continuous duty with the regular forces, or a person who, in accordance with the National Defence Act, accompanies the Canadian Forces, and the dependents of all such persons.

B   A person described in (A) of this section may make an application under Part III or Part IV of this Canon by forwarding his application to the Anglican Chaplain responsible for his pastoral care.

C   On receipt of an application mentioned in (B) from a person who is residing in Canada, the Chaplain shall forward the application to the Bishop of the Diocese in which the applicant is resident.

D   If the applicant is a person serving or residing outside Canada, the Chaplain shall forward the application to the Bishop Ordinary of the Canadian Forces for action.

E   Nothing herein contained shall prevent the making of an application by such a person in the manner prescribed by Part III or Part IV.

Notice of the application to the other party to a former union or questioned ceremony is required in certain cases, and notice may be given to any person whom the commission considers involved. Any person notified may appear or be represented and furnish information or make submissions.

Part VII
Forms

Forms for use in the administration of this Canon may be authorized from time to time by the National Executive Council of the General Synod.

Schedule A
Declaration

See **Part I, 2. and Schedule C, 5.**

We, _____ and _____, hereby declare that we intend to enter into marriage which we acknowledge to be a union in faithful love, to the exclusion of all others on either side for better or for worse, until we are separated by death.

We undertake to prepare ourselves for the exchange of vows at our wedding, recognizing that by this mutual exchange our union in marriage will be established.

We intend to strive thereafter to fulfill the purposes of marriage: the mutual fellowship, support, and comfort of one another, the procreation (if it may be) and the nurture of children, and the creation of a relationship in which sexuality may serve personal fulfilment in a community of faithful love.

Schedule B
Application for Declaration of Marital Status

See **Part III, 4 (A) & 6 (C), and Schedule C, 1.**

The following information must be provided so far as it is known:

1 The full name, and place of residence of the applicant.

2 The date and place of the marriage ceremony in question, its nature and form, by or before whom it was celebrated or solemnized, and the authority or purported authority of the celebrant.

3 The full name, and the place of residence if known, of the other party to the ceremony, at the time of the application.

4 The ages of the parties at the time of the ceremony, their then respective places of residence, domiciles and nationalities, their relationships towards each other by blood or marriage, whether either of them was under any disability or prohibition with respect to marriage generally or with respect to the other party, and the respective marital conditions of the parties immediately before the ceremony,

5 The proper law applicable to the ceremony and to the marriage otherwise than with reference to the ceremony, the relevant provision of the proper law or laws and authorities for such provisions,

6 Whether the requirements of the proper law or laws with respect to banns, licence or permit, to consent of parents or others, to examinations and other preliminary matters were duly complied with,

7 The alleged defects in the ceremony or in the marriage or purported marriage,

8 Whether (if relevant) either party has exercised any legal right to avoid the marriage or purported marriage or has approbated the marriage,

9 Full particulars of any proceedings in any court or ecclesiastical tribunal or commission in which the validity of the marriage or purported marriage was questioned directly or indirectly and the result of such proceedings,

10 Full particulars of any proceedings in any court or legislature or of any other act or event by which the marriage or purported marriage was or is alleged to have been dissolved or terminated.

11 Whether there have been children of the marriage or purported marriage and, if so, the full name, age, place of residence and present marital status of each child now living,

12 If any child of the marriage or purported marriage is a minor or under any disability or otherwise dependent on one or both of the parties to the marriage or purported marriage a statement showing who has the custody or is directly or indirectly responsible for the care and maintenace of the child and full details of present financial and other arrangements and future plans for the care, maintenance, education, and advancement of the child.

13 Where a male applicant has been a party to a ceremony of marriage with a woman now living, a statement showing what provision has been made and is being carried out for the present and future maintenance of the former wife or purported wife, or an explanation why there is no such provision,

14 Any other facts that would assist the Commission.

Schedule C
Application for Permission to Remarry According to the Rites of the Church

See Part IV, 1(C)

The following is required:
1   The information with respect to any prior marriage of either applicant with a person now living mentioned in Schedule B paragraphs 1, 2, 3, 4, 9, 10, 11, 12, 13 and 14,

2   A full explanation of the cause of the breakdown of the former marriage and the cause or grounds of dissolution or termination and of all efforts towards reconciliation and an explanation why no other efforts towards reconciliation were made,

3   A statement setting out the negotiations, if any, between the parties to the former marriage leading up to dissolution or termination,

4   Information necessary to enable the Commission to determine any question that must be determined under clause 2 of Part IV,

5   The Declaration set out in Schedule A, signed by both applicants,

6   Particulars of any previous application under Part IV made to any Ecclesiastical Matrimonial Commission.

Schedule D
Procedure of the Commission

See Part VI, 4.

1   Unless a marriage or purported marriage in respect of which an application is made has been civilly annulled or declared null and void or dissolved or terminated by a competent legislature or a competent court at the instance of or after due notice to the party thereto other than the applicant herein, the Commission shall before making a finding or determination cause the other party to be notified of the application in a manner that satisfies the Commission that the notice has been brought to the attention of the other party, if it is feasible to give such notice.

2   In any case the Commission may cause the other party to the marriage or purported marriage, or any other person whom the Commission believes to be concerned, to be notified of the application, if notification is feasible.

3   The notice shall be accompanied by a copy of the application and shall inform the person notified that he or she may assert or dispute any statement of fact,

submit evidence orally or in writing and make any submission or representation he or she sees fit to make in person or by representative.

4   Any statement, dispute, evidence, submission or representation made in response to the notice shall be communicated to the applicant who shall be given an opportunity of making answer or rebuttal.

5   Require proof of any additional fact which appears to be relevant to the matters involved in the application,

6   Require proof of any fact to be made by statutory declaration or to be made orally by affirmation, and require any document to be satisfactorily authenticated,

7   Require the applicant, in order to remove doubt, to take such proceedings in a competent civil court as may be necessary to establish or confirm the nullity of any purported marriage not already annulled or declared null and void by a court or legislature or the dissolution or termination of any marriage not dissolved or terminated by a court or legislature, or the competence in the premises of any court or legislature whose act, judgment or decree is relied on in relation to the marital status of the applicant,

8   Permit an applicant to be represented or assist by counsel or by a person having special skill and knowledge in canon law and pastoral care,

9   Make findings of fact based on any evidence satisfactory to the Commission, submitted in a matter satisfactory to the Commission, whether written or oral and direct or hearsay and whether or not verified by oath, affirmation or statutory declaration,

10 Conduct a hearing, if the Commission sees fit, in the presence of the applicant and of the other party to a marriage or purported marriage if the other party desires to attend, and of their representatives or assistants, or make a determination without a hearing if the Commission does not consider a hearing necessary, and no application for a hearing is made by the applicant,

11 Permit an application to be reopened or a fresh application to be made if further information is available after the Commission has disposed of an application.

Some Questions

Since it succeeded the former Commission on Marriage, the Sub-Committee on Marriage and Related Matters has responded to questions relating to interpretation of the Canon from the Ecclesiastical Matrimonial Commissions and from clergy and other interested persons. The questions and answers presented here are edited and arranged to correspond to the two preceding sections of the guide.

Who Officiates?

What is the status of non-Anglican applicants to the Matrimonal Commission?

According to the provisions of the Canon, it is the same as that of any other qualified applicant. The Canon in specific in not limiting applicants to Anglicans (Parts III, 3, (b) 1 & 2). The Canon also makes provision both for the marriage of baptized persons (without denominational reference), and for the marriage of a baptized person to one unbaptized (Parts I, 10 and II, 3).

While the Canon was being drafted, the commission was obliged to consider the question here addressed, and its eventual recommendation was quite specific as indicated above; this was confirmed by the General Synod in the adoption of the Canon. This view is virtually normative for Anglicanism wherever there is a parish system.

A parish priest is held responsible for the pastoral care of all who dwell within the physical boundaries of his parish. With the development of religious pluralism, since the sixteenth century in the West, the practice has of course been modified. The principle, however, of the availability of the pastoral care of all in the parish remains and is enshrined in the Anglican ordinal where the pastoral care of all is specifically referred to, most notably in the forms for the "Consecration of Bishops" and the "Ordering of Deacons."

In Anglican Canon law and in Prayer Book usage, a parish is a defined area where people dwell, and it includes all the people who live there (cf. Chapter 1).

In the pluralistic society of today, the solemnization of marriage is itself still an act of pastoral care, the value of which should never be underestimated. Parish priests still have the same potential responsibilities they have always had toward all who live in their parishes.

In our concern for couples, how do we relate to couples whom we do not know and will never see again?

Isn't it possible that their coming to the church for marriage may be the occasion for their entering or re-entering the life of the Christian community? The best should be hoped for, not the worst assumed in this kind of encounter (cf. Chapter 1). Some parishes involve married lay people in marriage preparation, an approach which involves such couples with members of the church other than the priest. Through this kind of apostolate, some couples will see the meaning of the Christian faith for their lives and make a fresh start as Christians. Others, realistically, will not. But this does not prohibit the incumbent from welcoming them with the same courtesy and interest with which he receives all those who come to him for marriage.

This meeting could provide opportunity for the priest to share with the couple the spiritual possibilities of marriage. Marriage can or ought to be the primary community of shared awareness or reflection on matters of life and faith. Also, the spiritual maturity of each individual shapes and influences the other, and therefore each one's journey to Christian maturity is inseparable from each other's journey.

The incumbent might also suggest to the couple the name of the local pastor in the community where they will be residing, in addition to forwarding their address to the pastor.

What does a priest do when he is asked to submit an application to remarry with which he doesn't agree?

a   If he believes the couple to be not suitable for remarriage, he still has the pastoral responsibility to help them to the best of his ability. He will forward their application to the commission together with his report stating his reservations. It is then his responsibility to inform the couple of these reservations. But it remains their right to have their application forwarded.

b   If, however, it is a question of his not agreeing with the remarriage of divorced persons *per se*, he is still required to inform the applicants that this is their right in the Anglican church. He forwards their application to the commission and facilitates their marriage by another priest providing the application is approved by the commission.

In this second instance, however, would not a priest who fundamentally disagrees with the church's remarriage of the divorced be well advised, as a pastor, to refer such couples immediately to another pastor who will prepare them personally and sympathetically? Still, if the couple insist, or if because of geographical reasons they have no choice, he is obliged to forward their application in any case.

What are the Rules?
Canon XXI with Commentary

Why does the Anglican Church of Canada make any canonical provision for the marriage to another person of one whose spouse is still living?

There are still today some inquirers who assume that it is self-evident that such regulation is unnecessary or even contrary to the Spirit of Christ. In the period 1965–1967, when the present canon was passing through the final stages leading to its adoption by General Synod, inquirers at that time would have been more likely to ask an opposite question: Why does the church allow any such marriage to be solemnized in the church at all? In the present period of cultural change both questions are live ones.

Until this century, the universal tradition of Anglicanism (embodied in its Prayer Books and Canons) was to forbid marriage in the church to a divorced person whose former spouse was still living. This rule is clearly and publicly stated in the third rubric, still printed without change in the current Canadian Book of Common Prayer, on page 563. The rule has a long history with its origin in the New Testament in words ascribed respectively to Christ and to St Paul.

> Whoever divorces his wife and marries another, commits adultery against her; and if she divorces her husband and marries another, she commits adultery (Mark 10:11f; cf. Luke 16:18).

> To the married I give charge, not I but the Lord, that the wife should not separate from her husband (but if she does, let her remain single or else be reconciled to her husband) — and that the husband should not divorce his wife (1 Corinthians 7:10f.).

From these and similar passages it was widely concluded that Christ himself had branded remarriage after divorce, while a former spouse was still alive, as an adulterous union (and one therefore forbidden by the seventh commandment). Hence, as St Paul confirmed, the proper course for a divorced person (whether guilty or innocent) was to remain single or else become reconciled to the former spouse. In simple justice it must be noted that countless thousands of Christians whose marriages had broken down have lived by this rule in faithfulness to what is here recorded as the teaching of Christ himself. Other thousands have conditioned their behaviour by this rule at least to the extent that, when they enter into new unions clearly in contravention of it, they are prepared to regard themselves as excommunicate. Grounds for exception have frequently been sought, and in more recent times grounds have been seriously considered by ecclesiastical authority. Part IV of the Canon continues this approach and limits it to certain defined cases.

Such then were the rules and such, in part, was the practice based upon them. This has been generally true of western Christendom for most of its history. What therefore has to be explained is why the Anglican Church of Canada finally decided to change the rules in 1967, and to do so in the conviction that the change was in full accord with the intent of the living tradition of faith in Christ. This conviction is set out in the preface of Canon XXI, where references are given not only to the origins of the tradition but to the changes which the apostolic church had already found itself obliged to initiate.

Background: Judaeo-Christian Tradition

Christian marriage law begin in Judaism with what "Moses commanded" (Mark 10:3). That law was interpreted by Jesus for his disciples in the circumstances of the Jewish community living in Palestine (Mark 10:5-9, etc.). It was shortly (and inevitably) interpreted further for the early Christian communities which grew up in Gentile society under Roman law (1 Corinthians 7:1-16, etc.). The process of change continued whenever radical cultural change made a fresh understanding of the tradition necessary in some new situation. For Anglicans, for example, marriage law assumed substantially its present form in the late feudal society of England in the sixteenth and seventeenth centuries (in the Prayer Books of 1549 and 1662 and the Canons of 1604). To describe the course of these changes is a task beyond our present purposes. Suffice it to say that such a study would have to conclude with an account of how contemporary urban-industrial culture

84

has come to affect our whole society, so that our perspectives are no longer those of the earlier and long-vanished paternalist and feudal culture reflected in seventeenth century Anglican documents.

It should be evident from these brief references that any Christian body (including the Anglican Church of Canada) must be prepared to give an account of itself if it should appear to permit what Christ is reported strictly to have forbidden. In doing so Anglicans continue the tradition of the church in the apostolic age which had already begun to formulate exceptions believed to be justified by the spirit of Christ made known to them and reflected in the fundamental teaching of the gospels. Two classic instances of this process, bearing on remarriage after divorce, are recorded respectively in 1 Corinthians 7:12–16 (in a Gentile culture) and in Matthew 19:9 (in a Jewish culture). Parts III and IV of Canon XXI are examples of a contemporary development of the same process, the aim of which remains unaltered: to be faithful to the intention of Christ. It is this process of development which is set out succinctly in paragraphs 3, 4, and 5 of the preface of Canon XXI.

What are the major mistaken assumptions about canon law?

An answer would seem to lie in the frequent confusion of canon law with the laws of civil society, especially in relation to its procedures.

Canon law is an instrument of the church's pastoral care of the people of God in their life in the church and in their mission to the world.

First of all, the canonical provisions for granting permission to applicants to be married in the church are not based upon evidence adduced in the civil proceedings. Nowhere does the Canon make any distinction between an "innocent" and a "guilty" party in the civil divorce. Nowhere is an ecclesiastical matrimonial commission authorized to review the civil proceedings, still less to make any judgment upon their civil effects. The Canon requires that the appropriate evidence must be produced to show that the applicants are *civilly free* to contract marriage; it must then on the basis of *other sorts* of evidence, rule on whether they may be married according to the rites of this church. For this, a commission must refer to the Canon law. In order to reach an affirmative decision it must be satisfied on the points listed in Part IV, 2; these may be conveniently summarized as follows:

a   That the marriage of an applicant whose former spouse is still living has in fact broken down. In establishing this, the commission is not authorized to pronounce any judgment about whose "fault" the breakdown may have been, nor does the commission have imposed upon it by the Canon any list of "faults," one or more of which must be shown to have caused the breakdown; rather, the breakdown must be judged by the commission to have been sufficiently clear and irreparable to justify granting the application. The commission must also be satisfied that reasonable efforts were made (if any were possible in the circumstances) to achieve reconciliation before the breakdown. The provisions are clearly designed for the sole purpose of establishing that what has occurred is real marriage breakdown and not either a frivolous separation or one unaccompanied by serious efforts at reconciliation, where such may have been possible.

b   That the applicants are both serious in their intention to co-operate in the exercise of either one's moral responsibility toward a former spouse or the children of a former union, where any of these may be in need and may have a moral claim for consideration by either spouse in the new marriage. As the exercise of this responsibility by one spouse making the application is bound to affect the new marriage, it is essential that both spouses co-operate in it.

c   That the applicants intend to enter upon marriage as it is understood by the church, at least one of the applicants being baptized.

The three provisions just summarized are pastoral in nature. They go well beyond the requirements of the civil procedure, and in their use of the concept of marriage breakdown they are to a large, though now decreasing, extent based on a different theory.

As we have said, canon law is an instrument of pastoral care. This does not mean that the canon law is uninterested in the civil effects of both marriage and divorce or in the appropriate sanctions related to these; but in this particular culture the church is content to leave judgments and sanctions in this sphere (e.g., distribution of property, and required family support) to the civil courts. The church's members are called to co-operate with all people of goodwill in establishing just laws in civil society (Canon XXI, preface, 8(H). We depend, wherever we can, upon the exercise of justice by the civil authorities, but beyond this the canon law is governed by faith in God's grace toward all humankind, especially in his offer of forgiveness, repentance, and the new life to all who are willing to accept them.

Preface

What is the relationship between the Matrimonial Commissions and common law marriages?

The Canon begins (preface 1) with a definition of marriage which is further developed in Part III, 2. This definition enables a commission to decide whether a relationship of cohabitation brought before it is or is not one upon which it may be competent to rule. For example, a commission might find that a purported marriage brought before it under Part III was in fact not a marriage as defined in the Canon. Nothing in the Canon can be construed as justifying the treatment of any form of permanent or temporary cohabitation as a marriage unless it conforms to the standard set forth in the preface which determines the sphere in which a commission is competent to judge. Apart from a commission's competence to make a judgment that a particular form of cohabitation does not constitute an impediment to marriage, in response to an application under Part III, the answer to the question posed is, none.

The various arrangements for temporary or permanent cohabitation which are common to most complex societies are subjects of concern to Christian teachers and pastors. Canon law is only one of the many instruments of pastoral care, and beyond its provision of definitions for the guidance of pastoral care, it cannot in the nature of things provide the substantial assistance needed in the cases under discussion. Pastoral care will be guided on the one hand by a Christian understanding of grace, morality, forgiveness, and perseverance, and on the other hand by the appropriate professional standards of interviewing, counselling, and therapy. A commission must from time to time advert to these competencies, for example when judging the adequacy of an incumbent's report upon an application. It is for reasons such as this that each commission is required to have among its members at least one person with competence in this field (Part VI, I (D)).

Is there more than one interpretation of the adultery passage? If so, what are they and how do they affect the interpretation of the Canon?

Yes, there are many interpretations of the adultery passage (Matthew 5:31, Mark 10:1–12, Matthew 19:3–12, Luke 16:18), too many to describe here. However, gospel commentaries on the passages indicated will give a variety of answers. A good article on the subject is that by Hugh Montefiore, "Jesus on Divorce and Remarriage," in *Marriage, Divorce and the Church* (London: SPCK, 1972), pp. 79–95. Bishop Montefiore concludes: "All will agree that Jesus taught that in the purposes of God marriage was meant to be permanent. Deliberately to cause or to contribute to the breakdown of marriage is, in Jesus's teaching, to go against the known will of God. Beyond this point, certainty ends." In other words, both in terms of the interpretation of these passages throughout Christian history, and in terms of their pastoral application, there has been wide disagreement. (See also F.W. Beare, *The Earliest Records of Jesus,* Oxford: Basil Blackwell, 1962, pp. 190–193.)

The Canon's interpretation is that Jesus, in these passages, was declaring the *intention* of God for the marriage of believers, not that he was *legislating.* The breakdown and legal dissolution of a marriage are, therefore, accepted as facts in an imperfect world in which the intentions of God are not yet fulfilled; and the marriage in the church of a person divorced from one who is still living is, therefore, not necessarily considered adulterous or bigamous.

Forgiveness applies to brokenness in marriage as it does to every other kind of situation. With the grace of God the future is open and a person is free once again to enter into a new relationship.

What does it mean when we say marriage is a sacrament?

In the wedding, God baptizes the couple's relationship in his love and power. Marriage thus becomes a visible and effective sign to society of the covenant between Christ and his church, God and his people. It symbolizes the unity God wills for all mankind (Preface, Par. 2). Marriage has the function of infusing, nurturing, encouraging, sanctifying, reconciling relationships in society. When Christians call their marriage sacramental, they are saying that they recognize the way in which those marriages do or do not show forth the intention of God for all people.

Part I Prerequisites for Marriage
Clause 2 Preparation

What resources are available to help increase the counselling skills of clergy preparing couples for remarriage?

Resources are too numerous to list. The problems for the clergy are where to find the time and financial support to make use of them. Any good training in counselling can be directed to the problems of a second marriage. Beyond this basic training the pastor will require only the appropriate knowledge of Christian doctrine and canonical procedure. The various forms of application to Matrimonial Commissions approved by the National Executive Council, and available from the Anglican Book Centre at nominal cost, offer guidance as to the areas of life and thought to be explored in counselling. The forms were drawn up specifically for this purpose and should be used as guides in counselling. It is suggested that every clergyman likely to be involved in procedures before a commission should always keep on hand a complete set of these forms.

The most important question, however, for the clergy is the availability of continuing education in counselling or other pastoral skills. For information about this, consult the Bursary Unit, Anglican Church House, 600 Jarvis Street, Toronto, Ontario M4Y 2J6, or the Canadian Association for Pastoral Education, 642 Beachollow Crescent, Mississauga, Ontario L4Y 3T2, or your nearest nationally accredited theological faculty, college, or seminary of any denomination, or (in some cases) a locally based training facility. If in doubt as to whether a training facility is responsibly organized, consult one of the two bodies just mentioned above for advice.

As to the availability of time and financial support for the clergy, there are now, both at the diocesan and national levels, various plans for study leave and financial support. It might be expected that one of the members of a commission designated as a person competent in the skills of pastoral care would be an appropriate commission member to assess the adequacy of an incumbent's report and, where it would be helpful, to assist an incumbent in finding opportunities for continuing education in this field.

How do clergy get training in order that they may be good pastors when interviewing couples applying for remarriage?

Some training is offered in theological colleges. It is mandatory in some, and optional in others. Requirements on this point also differ from diocese to diocese. In a general sense, clinical pastoral training is a good form of preparation for the kind of skills necessary to interview people applying for marriage or remarriage. If a priest has had no training of this kind, he can apply for funds and/or leave for continuing education in this field.

Another education opportunity, which is available to help clergy increase their effectiveness in ministering to remarried couples, is the marriage enrichment or marriage encounter movement. Clergy and their wives or husbands might consider choosing this kind of event in their continuing education program.

What is our response to couples who have been or are living together? Should we suggest they get married? How does it determine our marriage preparation?

a   The existence of couples living together outside formal marriage, a practice now rapidly increasing, constitutes both a challenge and a critique to the church and its understanding of marriage. It forces the church to reexamine and restate its view of what is essential in the man/woman relationship; and it criticizes the church's all-too-easy acquiescence in petrified and sterile marital patterns. At worst, of course, a couple who choose to live together may be indulging in regressive, immature, and selfish behaviour. At best, however, such a couple may be sincerely unable to enter a state which they have only seen in its anachronistic and repressive models. In many cases, living together represents the most that couples feel able to commit themselves to in an anxious and troubled society.

Our response to them, therefore, should be one of acceptance and willingness to enter into non-judgmental dialogue, whatever our private or theological view of the relationship. Contact with couples living in "alternative unions" can be a primary avenue of education, even evangelism, in both directions.

Essentially the same criteria apply to couples living together as to any others. They should get married if they want to and if they are ready to commit themselves to each other, in love, for life. They should not get married if they are not ready to make this commitment. Certainly the church should not be a party to persuading such couples to get married simply to legalize the relationship or otherwise make it "respectable." This would be as bad as persuading couples to marry simply to avoid the illegitimacy of an expected child, and would confirm to such couples their worst stereotypes of a church more interested in respectability than in honesty.

We can expect, perhaps (although not necessarily), to find it easier to discuss sexual matters with such couples. As far as communication goes, they will already have had experience of the kind of rough spots in daily life that may be still in the future for couples who have not lived together. But studies show that couples who have lived together do not necessarily have a better chance of forming an enduring union than couples who have not lived together. Therefore, what needs to be stressed more than anything is the nature and scope of the commitment to permanence and fidelity which is central to the Christian understanding of marriage.

Clause 5   Requirements of Civil Law

What authorities regulate the solemnization of marriage in the church?

General Synod prescribes the form of solemnization by the order of service of that name in the Prayer Book, which also forbids marriages within the degrees of kindred and affinity there mentioned. (Such marriages are invalid under civil law.) Marriage in the church is regulated by Canon XXI, of General Synod, bearing that title. The Prayer Book itself is authorized by Canon XIV of General Synod; the rubrics related to the form of "Solemnization of Matrimony" have, therefore, canonical effect, subject to the provisions of Canon XXI.

Subject to those provisions, the diocesan bishop has authority to regulate the solemnization of marriage within his diocese, by licensing clergy to minister therein, or granting permission to clergy who do not hold his licence to perform stated ministries which may include solemnization of marriage, regularly or occasionally. He also exercises pastoral and disciplinary oversight over this as well as other parts of the ministries of his clergy.

No person other than a cleric so licenced or permitted may solemnize marriage in our church (Part I, section 11 (B)).

The bishop may authorize appropriate modifications of the form of solemnization, where one of the parties is an unbeliever (Part II, section 3), as well as other modifications by virtue of his dispensing authority.

The appropriate bishop is authorized to confirm decisions of the appropriate Matrimonial Commission granting permission for the marriage in the church to a new partner of a divorced person whose former partner is living (Part

IV, and Part VI, section 1 (G)). Without that approval, solemnization of such a marriage by a minister of our church is forbidden (Part I section 9).

An individual minister may in his or her discretion refuse to solemnize a particular marriage (Part I section 11 (D)).

The consent of the incumbent of the parish is necessary to authorize a minister to solemnize a marriage in a parish to which he or she is not licensed (Part I section 11 (C)).

The civil and criminal law of Canada relating to marriage must also be complied with. Matters relating to solemnization, including preliminary requirements such as authority of solemnizer, licence or banns, medical examination, and consent of parents or others, are governed by the laws of the province or territory where the marriage is solemnized. Matters of capacity to marry, including mental capacity and being unmarried, consent of parties, prohibited degrees, and other elements of what is sometimes called "essential validity" are governed by the law in relation to such matters in force in the province or territory in which the parties are domiciled at the time of marriage. Perhaps the laws of two jurisdictions may be involved. In Quebec, that law is the Civil Code of the province and by that code absence of consent of parents or others, when required, creates incapacity to marry and is not merely a matter related to solemnization. In other provinces, the basic law is the law of England, but in one important matter the applicable law is not uniform in all jurisdictions. In Nova Scotia, New Brunswick, Prince Edward Island and Newfoundland, marriages within the prohibited degrees must be regarded as civilly valid unless dissolved or annulled. Elsewhere such marriages are absolutely null and void even without formal annulment, although courts may declare them to be so. Legislation relating to matters of "essential validity" can be enacted only by the Parliament of Canada, which has acted only to validate certain marriages formerly within the prohibited degrees.

Two offences relating to solemnization of marriage are created by sections 258–9 of the Criminal Code of Canada (Revised Statues of Canada, 1970, Chapter C–34) as follows.

258. Everyone who (a) solemnizes or pretends to solemnize a marriage without lawful authority, the proof of which lies upon him, or

(b) procures a person to solemnize a marriage knowing that he is not lawfully authorized to solemnize the marriage, is guilty of an indictable offence and is liable to imprisonment for two years.

259. Everyone who, being lawfully authorized to solemize marriage, knowingly and wilfully solemnizes a marriage in violation of the law of the province in which the marriage is solemnized is guilty of an indictable offence and is liable to imprisonment for two years.

The solemnization of marriage within the church is thus governed by two bodies of rules, those of the civil law and those of canon law and church discipline. Both bodies of rules must be complied with by ministers of our church.

Clause 10 Baptism

Why did the writers of the Canon stipulate that at least one person in the marriage be baptized? Does membership in the church have any significance at all in Christian marriage?

As the Canon states (Part I (10)), "The Form of Solemnization of Matrimony in the Book of Common Prayer is provided for the marriage of Christians." Here the Canon uses the word Christian to mean a baptized person, not necessarily a "committed" Christian.

Historically, since the church has seen itself as offering only the celebration of Christian marriage, baptism has been required. However, this has in many cases led to a perfunctory celebration of one of the great sacraments, which has thereby been reduced to a kind of technical prerequisite for getting married in church. As a result, first, of our increasing appreciation for the greatness of baptism in recent years, and second, of the increasing secularization of society, the whole matter needs to be rethought. The marriage of two non-Christians can be just as fully human a marriage as that of two Christians, but it is not a Christian or sacramental marriage.

Yes, membership in the church has significance in the community of Christians; baptism and grace are all significant for marriage. Membership in the church should mean that the couple has the care and support of a community committed to marriage and the well-being of married couples. Committed Christians being married today are in many cases asking their pastor to help them develop an authentic marital spirituality, recognizing that for them their marriage and family will be their primary Christian community. Marriage, after all, is an abiding form of Christian community, whereas in a highly mobile society all other communities — work, neighbourhood, congregation — are partial and transitory.

Why do we marry people who do not have a personal commitment to Jesus Christ?

Marriage was and is a human institution, "instituted of God in the time of man's innocency," and predating the church. It is a "given" in human society; and by helping people get married happily and responsibly, we can demonstrate to them that the church of Christ is interested in their welfare. It can be considered a kind of *praeparatio evangelica*, or preparation for the gospel. Every previously unknown couple coming to a priest to be married represents an opportunity to declare the good news of Christ. This can only be done if the couple somehow come to understand that God loves them, and is expressing his love for them through the church.

Part II The Solemnization of Matrimony

What obligations does Canon XXI impose on incumbents on officiating ministers relating to solemnization of marriages?

In what follows it is assumed that the officiating minister is also the incumbent. Where they are not the same, the officiating minister is referred to, unless the incumbent is expressly mentioned.

The Canon obliges the appropriate minister (1) to require at least 30 days notice before the day proposed for the wedding, except for grave cause, and to notify the bishop after each occasion on which he waives this requirement (Part I, section 1); (2) to require whether there are impediments to the marriage. These include

a Nonage. Each party must be at least 16 years of age, except for grave cause when permitted by provincial law and with prior approval and direction of the bishop (This requirement is canonical only);

b Mental defect or insanity depriving a party of capacity to give valid consent;

c Incapacity to consummate;

d Duress, coercion, or fear;

e Concealment by one party of venereal disease, or of addiction to drugs or alcohol, or of pregnancy except by the other partner, or of addiction to homosexual practices, sadistic conduct, or abnormal practice endangering the life or health of the other party (This requirement is canonical only);

f   Mistake with respect to the nature of the union or the identity of the other party;

g   Intention to go through the ceremony as a sham or mere form;

h   Kindred or affinity within the prohibited degrees listed on page 562 of the Prayer Book;

i   A subsisting marriage between one of the partners and a third person;

j   Any other impediment recognized by the civil law of the place of solemnization (Part 1, sections, 2, 3, 4 & 5, and Part III, section 2);

3   To ensure compliance with the civil law of the place of solemnization, relating to matters such as banns or licence, notices, consent of parents or others, medical examination, absence of prohibited relationship of kindred affinity, and so on (Part I sections 5, 6 & 7 and Part III section 2 (E));

4   To procure or secure appropriate means of education, so that the parties may come to marriage with a Christian understanding of its purpose and may be encouraged to give effect with God's help to the vows they are preparing to make;

5   To encourage the parties to read and sign the declaration prescribed by the Canon (Part I, section 2 and schedule A);

6   Not to solemnize a marriage where neither party has been baptized. Where only one has been baptized to refer the matter to the bishop and follow his order and direction (Part I, section 10);

7   Not to solemnize a marriage of two persons one of

whom has been a party to a ceremony of marriage with a third person now living except as provided in Part III or Part IV (Part I, section 9);

8   To solemnize the marriage in the body of the church, except for grave cause, and in the presence of at least two witnesses other than the officiating minister, and of the friends and neighbours who wish to attend. The words "body of the church" are currently interpreted by the majority of the House of Bishops to mean a part of the church building used by the clergy and members of the congregation for divine services, for example the chancel or nave or a chapel (Part II, section 1);

9   The incumbent is responsible for the conduct of the service, using only hymns or anthems found in the Holy Scriptures or the Prayer Book or Hymn Book or in texts approved by ecclesiastical authority (Part II, section 1);

10   To use modifications approved by the bishop when one party is an unbeliever (Part II section 3);

11   To make the entries and reports required by the civil authority and also in a parish register containing additional prescribed information (Part II section 4);

12   It is the incumbent's duty to complete, investigate, and forward to the appropriate Matrimonial Commission the prescribed application where permission is sought to marry in his or her parish after divorce while a former partner is living. The incumbent's own report must be included. The incumbent must seek the necessary information from others if he or she doesn't have it. The incumbent must recommend for or against permission and say whether, if permission is granted, he or she is willing to have the marriage celebrated in his or her parish (Part IV section 1 (B)).

Although the Canon does not deal with the problem, it is suggested that an incumbent who objects on conscientious grounds to remarriage after divorce while the former partner is living should refer the parties to another cleric who does not object, and allow the other to make all arrangements. The incumbent must nevertheless forward the application with his or her report, if the applicants require him or her to do so. If the incumbent recommends against approval because of his or her conscientious objection to such marriages and for no other reason, it is suggested that he or she should say so in the incumbent's report and ask the other cleric to attach his or her comments. If the incumbent does not consent to celebration of the marriage in his or her parish, the bishop will arrange where and by whom it is to be celebrated (Part III section 4 (1)).

Can a cleric of the Anglican Church of Canada evade compliance with Canon XXI or avoid use of the form of "Solemnization of Matrimony" on the ground that he or she is registered as a solemnizer of marriage under civil law and is, therefore, acting as an officer of the civil law and not as a minister of our church?

No. Canon XXI, which binds him or her since he or she is a minister of our church, requires the minister to comply with its provisions and the form of "Solemnization of Matrimony" as well as the civil law. The minister cannot say, "I am solemnizing a marriage out of the church as a civil officer" because he or she is not merely a civil officer. Moreover, he or she cannot in solemnizing a marriage cease to be a minister of our church and subject to its discipline, because he or she is not a civil officer except by virtue of and insofar as he or she is a minister of our church, and if he or she were not acting as a minister of our church he or she could not act in a civil capacity.

Except in Quebec, provincial and territorial legislation governing solemnization of marriage is essentially the same in relevant matters. Relevant provisions of the Civil Code of Quebec differ from legislation of other Canadian jurisdictions, but in practice the situation is essentially the same there as elsewhere in Canada, as far as our clergy are concerned.

In Ontario, authority to solemnize marriages is governed by sections 22–24 of The Marriage Act, Revised Statutes of Ontario, 1970, Chapter 261, as amended, relevant parts of which are as follows.

22. (1) No person shall solemnize a marriage unless he is a judge or a provincial judge, or is registered under this section as a person authorized to solemnize marriage.

23. No person shall be registered unless it appears to the Minister (of Commercial and Consumer Affairs, believe it or not):

(a) that the person has been ordained or appointed according to the rites and usages of the religious body to which he belongs . . .

(b) that the person is duly recognized by the religious body to which he belongs as entitled to solemnize marriages according to its rites and usages.

24. (1) Where it appears to the Minister that any person registered as authorized to solemnize marriage has ceased to possess the qualifications entitling him to be so registered or for any other cause, the Minister may cancel such registration.

(2) Every religious body, members of which are registered under this Act, shall notify the Minister of the name of every such member so registered who has . . . ceased to be associated with such religious body.

It will be seen from the foregoing that the only persons authorized to solemnize marriage other than by virtue of their status in a religious body are judges and provincial judges.

Members of our clergy authorized to solemnize marriages under Canon XXI are the only members of our church who may be registered under section 22(3), and when the minister is notified that one of them has ceased to be licensed or authorized, the minister will cancel the registration.

A member of our clergy, therefore, has no independent status or authority as a solemnizer of marriage by virtue of civil registration. Clerical authority is derived from orders and episcopal licence or permission, which extend only to solemnization according to the rites and usages of our church and under its discipline.

Part III
Determination of Marital Status
Clause 2   Conditions of Valid Marriage

What should a cleric do when he or she is asked to solemnize a marriage where a party has gone through a form of marriage with a third person which is alleged to have been invalid ("null and void")?

The minister is forbidden by Part I section 9 to solemnize the marriage unless the appropriate Matrimonial Commission has declared that the ceremony in question did not result in a marriage under Canon XXI and, therefore, does not constitute an impediment to marriage under the canon law of our church (or unless permission has been granted under Part IV).

The minister should inform the parties to that effect and invite them to apply under Part III for the appropriate declaration and assist them in preparing it.

In rare cases, Part III may be employed even though a marriage was civilly valid and has been terminated by divorce, if it suffered from a canonical defect mentioned in Canon XXI, as a result of which it was not entitled to be recognized as a marriage under the canon law of our church. In other cases, the former ceremony may have resulted in a civilly invalid marriage. There may have been a legal annulment or declaration of nullity; or there may have been no legal proceedings but the defect may have by pure operation of law prevented a valid marriage from resulting. In any event, the minister may not rely on the invalidity of the former ceremony until the appropriate Matrimonial Commission has declared that it has not created an impediment to the proposed marriage.

The parties should be advised to consult a lawyer if they have not already retained one in the matter. The minister should explain the requirements of Part III and Schedule B to the lawyer and the parties. If possible a legally qualified member of the Matrimonial Commission should be consulted. Together, all those concerned can make the necessary inquiries, obtain the necessary documents and, if required by Part III, section 4 (B) 4 and competent to do so, the lawyer can give an opinion on the validity of the former marriage. Such an opinion may have to be given by an expert in a foreign law.

The incumbent is required by Part III to receive the application, investigate it to the best of his or her ability, and forward it with the incumbent's report to the appropriate Matrimonial Commission. Since the question is one of canonical validity of the previous ceremony the minister is not required to make a recommendation.

Clause 6   Presumption of Death

Can a person whose spouse or former spouse is missing and believed to be dead, but who lacks absolute proof of the death, obtain permission to marry in the church?

Yes. In that situation, a civil divorce may but need not be obtained. Whether or not this has been done, an application may be made under Part III, section 6, for a declaration of presumption of death for canonical purposes.

Under the Criminal Code, section 254 (2) (a), a person does not commit the offence of bigamy in remarriage if he or she in good faith and on reasonable grounds believes that his or her spouse is dead. There is no civil law preventing such a person from regarding himself or herself as widowed.

In that situation, the canonical declaration of presumption of death permits remarriage in the church.

Part VI
Ecclesiastical Matrimonial Commission
Part VII   Forms

Why do all applications for remarriage, without exception, have to go to the Marriage Commission? Should the priest not have some discretion to grant permission to remarry in some cases?

The present system enables the minister to perform his or her work as pastor and counsellor while leaving the judgment with the commission. Since the commissioners depend on the quality of the relationship between the minister and the couple to make their judgment, both minister and commission should be seen as working together for the benefit of the applicant.

In some cases, should the judgment be left to the discretion of the minister?

At present, this is not permitted by the Canon. Some couples seemed to be blocked emotionally and psychologically from making a submission to a commission. No matter how well the minister relates to them in marriage preparation and explaining the purpose of the commission, they will go to another church rather than have an application for remarriage submitted to a commission. Yet order and discipline are important in these matters, as the church needs to maintain a consistent ministry to couples seeking marriage. This needs to be considered and re-thought.

Marriage belongs to the church and community. Remarriage, then, is of concern to the whole church, and this concern is symbolized by the role of the commission. Marriage is a local matter, but it is not only a local matter. This being so, part of the value of the commission is that it is removed from the pastoral situation.

Is it possible to explain more clearly the pastoral intention of the Matrimonial Commission and the forms?

The intention of the procedure governing Matrimonial Commissions is to ensure that the couple are ready for remarriage. Basically, this means two things. First, they are fulfilling their obligations to their former partners and are continuing to exercise their responsibility to their children. Secondly, they have prepared personally for their marriage. This means, in addition to preparation in terms of communication and spirituality, that they have worked through feelings about their former marriage (particularly the disappointment and grief that may be associated with that relationship). The forms are one way to gather the information that is necessary for the commission to make a fair judgment. It is important to remember that the forms should be used only after a relationship of trust and acceptance has been built up between the couple and the minister.

What defines the relationships between the applicant, the incumbent, and the commission with one another?

It has been suggested occasionally that a commission which has not seen an applicant cannot with propriety sit in judgment upon the application. This criticism misapprehends the procedure as this is set out in the Canon. Consider the steps of this procedure.

a   The applicant seeks the appropriate incumbent. (For this, see the previous section.) "The application shall be made to the incumbent. . ." (Part IV, 1 (b), or also Part III, 3(c), 2);

b   "The incumbent shall investigate the application to the best of his ability and forward it together with his report . . . to the Ecclesiastical Matrimonial Commission . . ." (Part IV, 1 (B); cf Part III, 3(C)). The incumbent provides the required facts and offers the Commission his or her considered pastoral judgment;

c   The commission: "Each application shall be dealt with as expeditiously as possible." (Part VI, 5). The commission is to proceed as described in Schedule D. An applicant may appear before the commission (Schedule D. 3, 4, 8 & 10); but the commission is given no powers to require such appearance as a condition for its decision;

d   The decision: the commission makes a finding and declaration of marital status under Canon law (if acting under Part III), or grants or refuses permission to marry in the church (if acting under Part IV);

e   The bishop: The decision, to become effective, requires confirmation by the diocesan bishop. (While this assumes that confirmation might be withheld, the bishop is not given the power to reverse a decision. This is an important feature of the Canon for the protection of the bishop, a subject to which we return in the concluding paragraphs of this section);

f   The registrar of the commission shall "communicate each decision to the appropriate incumbent and the applicants or applicant. . ." (Part VI, 1 (H)).

106

Is the Commission merely a rubber stamp?

The question arises because the dismissal of an application seems to be a comparatively rare event. There is, however, no reason to doubt that this is one of the beneficial results of the interviewing and pastoral counsel which precede the submission of an application. In the course of the preliminary counsel with the incumbent, it may become very clear to an applicant that a proposed application would be inappropriate, so that in such a case it will be withdrawn at this stage and will never reach the commission. If, on the other hand, interview and counsel should lead to a mutual agreement that an application is sound and worthy of consideration according to the canonical provisions, it will be forwarded to the commission. In these circumstances it would not seem strange if it were then granted for the same reasons which emerged during the pastoral interview. The high proportion of applications granted is surely the result we might expect. The Sub-Committee on Marriage and Related Matters has seen no reason to doubt that it is the result of the pastoral work involved, nor to doubt that pastoral care is being given where it belongs — in the parish.

The commission is far from being a rubber stamp. It provides an unbiased voice of authority serving as a sanction for the work of pastors who must deal with difficult marital situations; it sanctions the drawing of a line to determine the minimum standards that can be embraced within the pastoral care of marriage.

How are Commissioners and ministers assured that the information they receive is correct?

The method of assurance open to Commissioners is described in Schedule D. The method of seeking assurance open to incumbents is dependent in part upon their ordinary pastoral skill and in part upon their following the procedures clearly set out in the forms for making the incumbent's report. It does not seem possible to say more than this without entering upon a discussion of the nature of pastoral interviewing and counselling, of the dynamics of such a process, and of the care and compassion required to bring it to an effective conclusion. There appears to the Sub-Committee on Marriage and Related Matters to be no way in which such a process and such a skill could be imposed by Canon. At present the church has no generally adopted plan for ensuring that her pastors are qualified to practice in the way that the other two ancient professions provide teaching facilities and tests to qualify for practice.

What is the procedure for couples applying to the Matrimonial Commission who live in another diocese? For example, if a couple live in Toronto and wish to be married in Nova Scotia, to what commission do they apply?

In the example given, they apply to the incumbent of the parish in Nova Scotia in which they wish to be married. The incumbent presents the application with his or her report to the Nova Scotia commission. This is set out clearly in the Canon, Part IV, 1 (B). If the incumbent does not know the couple or does not know one of them, he or she is directed to secure the relevant information to the best of his or her ability from a former pastor or pastors of the couple or from others having knowledge of the facts. This too is clearly set out in the authorized form in the prefatory notes on the first page of the form.

Who is responsible for evaluating the effectiveness of the Matrimonial Commission?

The responsibility in question has not been assigned by the General Synod to any person or group.

The Sub-Committee on Marriage and Related Matters receives reports from all commissions, and gross disparities, if any, would probably show up in these reports. The sub-committee seeks to co-ordinate information for possible use in the event that some change might seem to be called for.

The subject of possible disparities among the commissions was often raised in the Commission on Marriage and Related Matters when the Canon was being drafted. The subject is raised again here. This may serve to remind Anglicans once again of a historic constitutional problem, the solution of which lies beyond the competence and terms of reference of this sub-committee. Within the whole Anglican communion there is a diocesan system which always exists in some tension with Anglican provincial, national, and international organization. To assert the superiority of some national body over the work of the commissions, however desirable such a course might seem to some, was not a course which the commission was prepared to recommend to the General Synod for incorporation into canon law. The practical resolution of the problem as adopted in the Canon may be seen in Part IV, 3 and in Schedule D, 7. A diocesan or provincial commission is itself the final court of appeal. Should disparities be judged by this sub-committee to constitute an injustice requiring redress, it would be open to the sub-committee to make an appropriate recommendation in its report to the General Synod.

What are the standards for membership on a commission?

They are laid down in Part VI, 1 (D).

The reason for at least one qualified lawyer on the commission is that the commission must have a member qualified to explain the civil effects of any event or proceeding touching upon an application before the commission; see, for example, Part III, 2 (A), 3 (b); Part II, 2 (E); Part III (6) A; Part IV, 1 (A).

The requirement that at least one person qualified in canon law should be on each commission is to establish assurance that proceedings before a commission will be governed by the principles appropriate to canonical legislation and will not become dominated by rules more appropriate to civil or criminal procedures; see, for example, Schedule D, Procedure of the Commission, passim, and especially paragraphs 3, 8, and 9.

The reason for at least one person skilled in pastoral care is to establish assurance that the proceedings are conducted as an element in the pastoral care of the church for her people, a care which has always in mind the world of grace, forgiveness, and redemption as well as the potential support of the pastor and the Christian community in the continuing life of the parties. In this is to be seen one of the historic differences between the canon law and the civil law. The canon law has always contained a large element of doctrine and teaching, an element which is sometimes difficult for persons whose professional training has been in other systems of law to take account of in legal proceedings under the canon law.

It would appear from questions addressed to this subcommittee by various commissions from time to time that they identify insufficient knowledge of canon law and poor access to an adequate quality of pastoral care as being among the major problems which commissions encounter in their work.